The Life of
Thomas Hayton Mawson
Landscape Architect
1861-1933

By Elizabeth Kissack

With Best Wishes
Elizabeth Kissack

Also Author of 'A Cumberland Vicar's Daughter'
The story of the life of Eliza Lynn Linton.

For my family

Left: Lake at Wren's Nest, Grasmere.

Copyright © Elizabeth Kissack 2006

Published by
Elizabeth Kissack, 9 St John's Gardens, Lake Road, Windermere, Cumbria LA23 2FD
Tel. 015394 47768

All rights reserved. No part of this publication may be reproduced, stored in any retrieval system, or transmitted, in any form, or by any means, electronic, mechanical, photocopying, recording or otherwise, without prior permission of the publisher and copyright holder.

Elizabeth Kissack has asserted moral right to be identified as the author of this work.

ISBN 978-0-9553653-0-0

All photographs by Elizabeth Kissack unless otherwise acknowledged.
Black and white photographs by permission.

Printed by Stramongate Press Ltd, Aynam Mills, Little Aynam, Kendal LA9 7AH

ABOUT THE AUTHOR

Elizabeth Kissack, or Bette, as she is more widely known, has a profound interest in many aspects of Lake District history. As well as having worked voluntarily on the Beatrix Potter Archive of Botanical paintings for the Armitt Library in Ambleside she spends much time at the Lakeland Horticultural Society's Gardens at Holehird which have both Beatrix Potter and Thomas Mawson connections.

Her interest and research into the life and works of Thomas Mawson led to an invitation to give two lectures on him to the Lakeland Horticultural Society. She has, since then, become recognised as the local authority on the subject and is very much in demand as a speaker. She has lectured on Thomas Mawson to National Park Landscape Gardening students at Brockhole, the Headquarters of the Lake District National Park, History Societies and Civic Societies. Her lectures are also given to Women's Institutes and Probus Clubs, Gardening clubs and Horticultural bodies.

As Mawson's autobiography has been out of print for almost eighty years, this book is an attempt to satisfy the demands of Bette's various audiences who want more information than she can fit into one, or even a series of lectures.

This book is also Bette's tribute to a man who not only left his mark on gardens and houses in the English Lake District but all over the British Isles and in Holland, Denmark, Greece, America and Canada, over a period of forty years. She found Mawson's life so incredible that she was moved to put it into print for others to discover and enjoy.

Bette, in the gardens at Holehird where she is the official photographer and a member of the small team that curates the National Collection of Hydrangea.

Photograph by Margaret Thomas

Sources of Information

Jolly, W.P. Lord Leverhulme. Constable. 1976.
Smith, M.D. Leverhulme's Rivington. Wyre Publishing, 1998.
United Utilities Information Leaflets, Great House Information Centre,
    Rivington, Bolton. Special thanks to Sue Harper.
Chorley Borough Council, Rivington Terraced Gardens Project.
Barrow Borough Council, Barrow-in-Furness.
This England. The Register of the Victoria Cross. The Bath Press Limited, 1997.
Anthony H. Gaddum. Gaddums Revisited. The Amadeus Press, 2005.
Mawson, T.H. & E.P. The Art & Craft of Garden Making. Batsford Press. 1926.
Mawson, T.H. The Life and Work of an English Landscape Architect.
The Richards Press. 1926.
Quotations in italics taken from this source.

Contents

Chapter 1	In the Beginning	1
Chapter 2	Grand Lakeland Mansions	5
Chapter 3	The Practice Expands	18
Chapter 4	New Year, New Works	21
Chapter 5	Family Affairs	24
Chapter 6	The Golden Years	27
Chapter 7	Light and Shadow Along the Way	32
Chapter 8	A Friendship Leads to America	36
Chapter 9	More Travel Abroad	38
Chapter 10	Welcome Return to the Lake District	40
Chapter 11	The History of Wood Hall	46
Chapter 12	Lecturing in the USA and Canada	49
Chapter 13	Britain with a Hint of Japan	51
Chapter 14	Return to America and Canada	59
Chapter 15	A Fortuitous Meeting, and the Antipodes Postponed	63
Chapter 16	Comings and Goings 1913-1914	66
Chapter 17	The War Years	69
Chapter 18	'Cometh the Occasion, Cometh the Man'	74
Chapter 19	The 'Storey' of the Westfield Military Village, Lancaster	79
Chapter 20	Mawson in Greece	85
Chapter 21	With Lord Leverhulme in the Hebrides	88
Chapter 22	The Armistice	91
Chapter 23	Changes in 1920	96
Chapter 24	The Final Years	99

Some of the one hundred strong workforce employed by Lord Leverhulme to create Mawson's gardens on Rivington Pike, near Bolton.

Forty of the craftsmen empoyed on creating Mawson's gardens at Wood Hall near Cockermouth, Cumberland.

Photograph courtesy of Dorothy & Jack Jackson, Wood Hall, Cockermouth.

Chapter 1

IN THE BEGINNING

On 5th May, 1861, Thomas Hayton Mawson was born in the picturesque village of Scorton, eight miles south of Lancaster. He was born to parents who had passed with great courage and fortitude through a period of the cotton famine which had proved the ruin of so many families involved in, and relying on, the Lancashire cotton mills for employment.

His father, John William Mawson, had been born at Halton, just outside Lancaster, and was lucky enough to gain a sound English education thanks to Dr. Mackereth, the rector of Halton, who was a distant relative. It was he who taught John William not only good English but Latin and algebra, and also gave him a love for good literature. Dr Mackereth's kindly influence remained with John William throughout his life. Although brought up as an Anglican, with sincere regard for his rector, John William soon came under the influence of nonconformity, to which he brought a fine lovable character, a well-stored mind, a charm of address and an appealing musical voice and unquestioned sincerity. He would have made an ideal rector, himself. However, circumstances drove him into business for which he was not really suited.

Thomas's mother Jane, (nee Hayton) was of a very different temperament,…practical, proud, alert, and very ambitious for the success of her children. In her youth she had enjoyed a reputation as a public speaker. Even through illness, she would not relinquish her five young children. Thomas and his siblings adored their father and feared their mother who was the one to dole out any punishment she thought necessary. In their maturity, however, the children realised their mother, when head of the family, had a wonderful personality too.

From a very young age Thomas unconsciously developed powers of observation and a very good memory, faculties which never left him. By the time he was twelve years old he knew where to find every old door-head, date-stone, sundial, quaint gateway, oriel or mullioned window, for miles around his home.

He was destined to become a landscape architect of world renown, working all over Britain, Canada, America, Denmark, and Greece. He won the international competition to design the gardens surrounding the Peace Palace in The Hague. He worked for Kings and Queens, Dukes, Lords and Viscounts and many of the rich industrialists of the early twentieth century.

When Thomas was six years old, his family moved to Lancaster where his father's brothers were in business as builders. His father bought a plot of land on which he built a pair of semi-detached houses, one of which the family occupied. It was at this time that Thomas got his first taste for gardening. Being a rather delicate child, he was put to work on the garden as his parents thought that the fresh-air and exercise would do him good and he was first taught how to dig a straight line. From digging he soon progressed to planting and sowing and his life-long love of gardening had begun! He spent his few pennies of pocket money on packets of seeds, recalling how he liked to buy packets of candytuft, mignonette, virginian and ten-weeks stocks and clarkias, before he graduated on to growing vegetables.

It was not long, however, before the family moved again, much to Thomas's sorrow at leaving his garden, to live in Ingleton, where his father had secured a position. They rented at first a quaint old whitewashed cottage with mullioned windows, and with one of those carved door-heads peculiar to that locality. John William soon chafed at being under a landlord, and very soon purchased ground on which to build a cottage.

Here, Thomas attended the Church school in the village between the ages of nine and twelve. Fortunately, the young schoolmaster was a man of character, Samuel Coburn by name, who devoted endless time and patience to his pupils, and Thomas in particular, to whom he took a liking . Thomas managed during this time to rise two forms or standards each year. Thomas always thought of Samuel Coburn as his ideal gentleman, and one to whom he would be forever grateful.

When he was twelve years old, he started work as an office boy to one of his builder uncles, who was also a keen horticulturist. He lived in Lancaster and took Thomas into his home for two years, until his own father needed him again. There he learnt the preparation of working drawings and the use and quality of building materials. Included in his duties would be to make tracings of contract drawings and keep a check on materials sent to buildings in course of construction. In fact, the work constituted the best technical training he could have ever have had. In the evening, he pursued serious study in drawing at the Lancaster Mechanics Institute.

At the age of fourteen, it was practically decided that he should enter the designing department of the old, respected, Lancaster firm of Gillows, but his father moved the family yet again, this time to Langber End, midway between Ingleton and Bentham, where he wanted to start a nursery and fruit farm. He needed his boys, Thomas and younger brother Robert, who was now twelve and a half years old, to double-trench the land. This the boys were very willing to do.

Alas, after only two years, their father died, a very great sorrow in Thomas' life. After eighteen months of struggle, their mother decided they must sell-up and Thomas must go to London and find work for himself and for his brothers. This he did, very quickly, and sent for his two brothers, Robert and Isaac, his mother and sister, Sarah.

In London came Thomas' introduction to practical commercial horticulture, working for several Nurserymen of good repute, the first being John Wills with whom he stayed for two years, always starting work at six a.m. Disaster fell once again, when the Wills business went into liquidation.

Thomas was, by now, close upon twenty-one years of age and was fortunate to find employment with Thomas S. Ware, of Hale Farm Nurseries, Tottenham. He worked hard and conscientiously and was soon promoted to be in charge of the firm's extensive correspondence. Through this, he was in touch with notable people, such as Gertrude Jekyll. He was soon travelling within a fifty miles radius of London, visiting the firm's wholesale customers. He became acquainted with a well-known firm of nurserymen on the Surrey side of the river and was offered a partnership on advantageous terms. Being now twenty-three, he considered this would further his plans for the practical application of his own ideas on garden design and for finding a wife to settle down with.

Every afternoon, on his way home from work, he passed by the London Fever Hospital, in Tottenham, and every day, about the same time, a particular night-nurse would be walking to the hospital. They were much too "proper" to notice one another, of course, but both began to wish that *someone* would introduce them! One day she failed to appear but, as Thomas passed the hospital, he saw her at an open window rearranging a vase of half-dead flowers for the children's ward.

This was too much for the young horticulturist, who called out: *"Nurse, you cannot make anything decent out of those flowers; allow me to bring you some fresh ones!"* She accepted his offer and the rest was inevitable. The nurse was Anna Prentice, daughter of a Norfolk Surgeon, the late Dr. Edward Prentice. They were married within six months, on 1st August, 1884, at Trunch Church, Norfolk. They honeymooned in the Lake District.

During their honeymoon, Thomas received a letter from the Surrey nurseryman with whom he was negotiating a partnership, saying that the partnership had fallen through. After the initial disappointment, on looking round, Thomas and Anna decided to take the plunge and start a family business in the Lake District! The more they saw of the district, the more they liked it and became convinced that their idea could become a success. Before leaving the area, they informed a local estate agent of their needs. This was in August 1884 and, in the following January, they were informed that a suitable site had been found with almost an acre of land, at a reasonable rent, on a long lease. They telegraphed the agent to close and, in another five weeks, in February 1885, the Mawson Brothers, their mother, and Thomas's wife, established themselves in Windermere, at the New Road Nursery. They set to work to make a survey of the nursery site and to plan new offices, propagating houses and frame yards. Their programme was to establish a nursery and contracting business for Robert and Isaac and for Thomas to obtain, as a member of the firm, all the landscape gardening he could get hold of, but to separate the professional practice from the nursery business directly they were both established. This separation took place in 1889.

The Life of Thomas Hayton Mawson

The Mawson Brothers L to R: Isaac, Robert and Thomas

Some time later, Thomas acquired a separate Drawing Office in Windermere, *"of which I became very fond"*, he said. *"It consisted of two larger rooms, my own and the drawing office, together with a third queer, irregular box-like place at the rear, which was used by my book-keeper and private secretary, and was where I did much of my best work."*

Chapter 2

GRAND LAKELAND MANSIONS

Mawson's very first commission to landscape a garden was at Far Sawrey, for a Mr.Bridson, (pronounced Brideson), who was just completing a large house, 'Bryerswood', designed by the well-known Bolton architect Knill Freeman who also designed the new additions to Graythwaite Hall. Mr. Bridson had previously lived in the Round House on Belle Isle, the largest of the islands on Windermere, where he kept a flock of St. Kilda Sheep and held Sheep Dog Trials on the Island. The commission came about, for Thomas, when he received a letter from Mrs. Arthur Severn, a distant cousin to John Ruskin, (although Thomas thought her to be Ruskin's niece), of 'Brantwood', Coniston, to say she had recommended him to Mr. Bridson, who wanted advice on the laying out of his garden on the western side of Windermere. Thomas lost no time in seeing Mr. Bridson and submitting his designs. Within a few days, he had made his survey and prepared a preliminary plan of the prospective gardens. The plan was carefully studied by Mr. and Mrs. Bridson, especially in relation to the commanding view obtainable across Windermere, embracing the landscape on the other shore of the lake. (Just a few years later, 'Blackwell', the Arts and Crafts house, was built on the eastern shore of Windermere directly opposite Bryerswood. Mawson was to be engaged there too, in landscaping its grounds).

Photograph by kind permission of Mr. & Mrs. S. Crabtree.

Bryerswood demolished 1956/57

Immediately after the Bridson's had accepted his plans, and the estimate of costs, work commenced, all within a fortnight. Thomas recalled, *"I secured a splendid old fellow as foreman, one of the old-fashioned school, thoroughly versed in constructional garden work, hard working, and loyal. Old Kidd stayed with us as long as he could work, and we never lost money on any contract carried out under his superintendence."*

After only two days, Mr. Bridson gave Thomas a cheque for £200 saying, *"When you want more, let me know!"* That cheque was a godsend and a boost to the morale of the Mawson Brothers who, from then on, went from strength to strength. (Sadly, Bryerswood was demolished in 1956/57, but Mawson's very large Walled Garden still exists.)

Mawson's walled garden which was constructed for Bryerswood

Whilst working at Bryerswood Mawson met, for the first time, the Bolton architect Knill Freeman and it was here that Thomas first met Captain Bagot, who had just inherited Levens Hall, and many were the talks they had about the Captain's quaint world-famous Topiary gardens. Here, also, was a very important introduction to Col. Sandys, M.P., who invited him to improve the gardens and park at his home, Graythwaite Hall. During the time spent at Graythwaite, Mawson came to regard Col. Sandys with a great respect. At the time his services were requisitioned, the Colonel had been in possession of the property for seventeen years, spending the entire rent roll and more on the estate, which extended from two miles north of Lake Side Station to and comprising most of the village of Hawshead, a distance of at least six miles. The entire area of Esthwaite Lake and a part of each of the two villages of "Sawrey Infra" and "Sawrey Ultra" were included. Today, these villages are known as Near Sawrey and Far Sawrey. The Colonel was most conscientious in the responsibilities of his position and exercised over his estate a kindly

Graythwaite Hall Garden

paternalism. He paid fees to a doctor to provide medical attendance for the whole estate, when required.

On completion of the garden design, which gave ample scope to Thomas's passion for terraces and balustrades complemented by a wealth of ball-finials, Mawson visited the work at Graythwaite three days a week, driving in all weathers, summer and winter, in a small open trap. Becoming more like a friend than an employee, Thomas asked him, one day, did he ever regret all the money he had spent on the estate in the last twenty years? *"Never!"* the Colonel replied, *"A brother officer of mine also spent £120,000, as I have done,…but on horse-racing, so I pride myself I have made the better choice."* Thomas showed his admiration for Colonel Sandys by dedicating one of his first books on garden design to the great man. At Graythwaite, Thomas had met architect Dan Gibson, who designed the tall, columnar sundial in the Dutch Garden, an ornate wooden bridge to cross the small stream in the grounds and ornate iron gates at the rear of the Hall. Mawson worked closely with Gibson for the next two years. (The wooden bridge was replaced by a stone bridge in 1937).

Another occasion at Graythwaite was to bring more work for Mawson when he was introduced to George Gregory, a well-known Parliamentary solicitor and legal adviser to Colonel Sandys. Mr. Gregory was at the time building Riverside, near Staines, and asked Mawson to lay out the gardens, at some future date. This was to be Thomas's first commission at any distance from home.

A huge commission for Mawson and Gibson to work together was

The Life of Thomas Hayton Mawson

The Dutch Garden, Graythwaite Hall, with Sundial by Dan Gibson, centre path

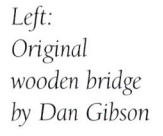

Left: Original wooden bridge by Dan Gibson

Right: Original Ornate Gate designed by Dan Gibson at Graythwaite Hall

Left: Top of Sundial pillar at Graythwaite Hall designed by Dan Gibson

Right: Graythwaite Hall and grounds

Grand Lakeland Mansions

Brockhole, 1899-1900, for W. H. A. Gaddum, Esq., 'a Manchester man with a passion for Lakeland'. Gibson was entirely responsible for the design of the house, whilst Mawson was entirely responsible for landscaping the garden, grounds, plantations and entrance drives.

In 1886, William Henry Adolphus Gaddum (always known as Willie) had married Edith Elizabeth Potter. She was the daughter of Walter Potter, the brother of Rupert whose famous daughter, Beatrix Potter was the author of the now famous children's books about Peter Rabbit, Jeremy Fisher, Jemima Puddleduck and company. The girls were double cousins as their fathers and mothers were brothers and sisters.

The Potter brothers controlled a large concern of calico printers and were an influential family in Manchester at that time.

Willie had been educated at Uppingham School, as were Canon Hardwicke Drummond Rawnsley, one of the founders of the National Trust, and his brother Willingham Franklin Rawnsley, MA.

Willie and Edith both had a strong love of the Lake District, Willie, because during his youth, his family on more than one occasion had taken a house at the head of Windermere known as 'The Croft'. Here Willie was introduced to yachting, a sport which held a fascination for him throughout life. Photography was another passion of his, for which family and historians will be ever grateful. The Gaddums filled eleven huge albums with photographs and Willie recorded on film every stage of the building of Brockhole beginning with the digging-out of the footings. After their marriage Willie and Edith maintained contact with the Lake District by taking a house, Sawrey Knotts, on the western shore of Windermere. Coincidently, Sawrey Knotts neighboured with Bryerswood where Mawson had landscaped the garden for Mr. Bridson, Thomas's very first commission of his Landscape Gardening career. At this same time Dan Gibson was working as an architect at Graythwaite Hall, also a close neighbour to Sawrey Knotts. It would be here that Mr. Gaddum became aware of these two men. Eventually, when Willie decided to have his own house built in the Lake District, Dan Gibson was given the contract as architect to build Brockhole and Thomas Mawson was commissioned to landscape the 32 acres of grounds on the lakeside between Ambleside and Windermere, belonging to the house. Brockhole became the Gaddums permanent home from 1900, where they were to spend the rest of their lives.

Whilst living at Brockhole, Willie was able to indulge in another of his passions which was a fascination with the technique of lathe-work, in which art he was to become a recognised authority. A complicated box he made was immediately recognised as his work at a meeting of the Worshipful Company of Turners fifty years after his death.

Willie and Edith had two children, Walter Frederick, always known as

The Life of Thomas Hayton Mawson

Digging out the footings Brockhole 1899

Mrs Gaddum inspecting the work

Mawson, right, explains his garden plans at Brockhole to Mr & Mrs Gaddum

Photographs by permission of the National Park, Brockhole.

Grand Lakeland Mansions

Brockhole, House and Terrace today

Left: Brockhole from the second terrace

Bottom Left: Dan Gibson's Summerhouse, Brockhole

Right: Dutch Garden, Brockhole

11

Jim, and Elizabeth Margery, always known as Molly, which can be quite confusing to people outside of the family. Brockhole remained in the Gaddum family for forty-five years.

An anecdote told by Beatrix Potter's housekeeper Mrs. Rogerson, many years later, `relates that *"the last occasion for which Beatrix, (now Mrs. Heelis) had worn her jewels was for Mr. and Mrs. Gaddums' Golden Wedding celebration in February, 1936. For this, Beatrix had worn a tight silk dress with buttons down the back. When she returned home, being now rather stout, she found she was unable to undo the buttons; so spent the night sitting in a chair in her bedroom. Mrs. Rogerson released her from the dress when she arrived next morning."*

Mr. Gaddum photographed every stage of the laying out of the garden by Thomas Mawson.

Gibson and Mawson had great respect for one another but realised that their interests were so varied and each so successful in his own field that they regretfully dissolved their two year partnership to go their own ways. They always remained friends. In fact, Mawson's second son became a pupil in Gibson's office the following week.

The work at Bryerswood, Graythwaite and Brockhole led almost immediately to the Mawson firm being employed by others in the Lake District, including some work for Sir Henry Moore, K. C. B., of Crook. Thomas later said *"Sir Henry was the most lovable old gentleman I have ever met and as picturesque as he was lovable. At ninety, the old man would walk to Windermere and back, a distance of four miles each way, with a spring and a swing which put to shame many a man half his age."* The work at Crook was to extend lawns and walks round the new additions which had recently been built to the family home, adding a few rose beds and a little planting along the boundaries to emphasise the vistas. Sir Henry was noted for his many sage and quaint observations. When at the end of the work, Thomas remarked that the cost was more than he had anticipated, he replied, *"You are a young man: take the advice of an old one. Whenever you have to choose between a big expenditure coupled with a good job, and a small expenditure with a bad one, choose the first…the pain of paying the account is momentary; the satisfaction with the work is permanent. A bad job is quickly paid for, but the dissatisfaction with the work is lasting, and you will find that your client will forget how little of his money you spent, but curse you eternally as a bad workman."*

Around 1897, Mawson had been called to Holehird, the home of William Grimble Groves, to create glasshouses in the walled garden in which Mr. Groves could indulge his passion for growing orchids, flanked on either side by peach houses and vineries. These glasshouses were demolished in the late 1970's.

Grand Lakeland Mansions

Other grand houses in the immediate area with gardens landscaped by Mawson at the turn of the 19th century, include Cringlemire, for Mr. Henry Martin, a Halifax Manufacturer. This is a large country house on the high road between Ambleside and Troutbeck, the original part of the house being built in 1861. The Yew hedging and archways created by Mawson, c 1900, and decorative ball finials all around the garden, still exist today. Dan Gibson designed the Summer House.

Above Left:
Cringlemire in its beautiful setting.

Above Right:
Mawson Arch at Cringlemire.

Left:
Yew hedging to Mawson's original plan at Cringlemire.

Photograph by Rod Davies

At the lakeshore mansion, Langdale Chase, Mawson designed a balustraded terrace from which to view the magnificent lake and mountain scenery, and a majestic stone staircase sweeping down to give panoramic views of the lower garden and grounds spread below. This is a wonderful example of blending the garden with the house. The pathway then becomes a decorative small bridge with an abundance of small ball finials edging the sides to cross a small beck running into the lake. On reaching the beautiful boathouse, designed to match the house in perfect harmony, the lakeside path gives a superb view of the Lakeland Hills, in particular, Crinkle Crags and the Langdale Pikes.

Langdale Chase Garden looking up to the house

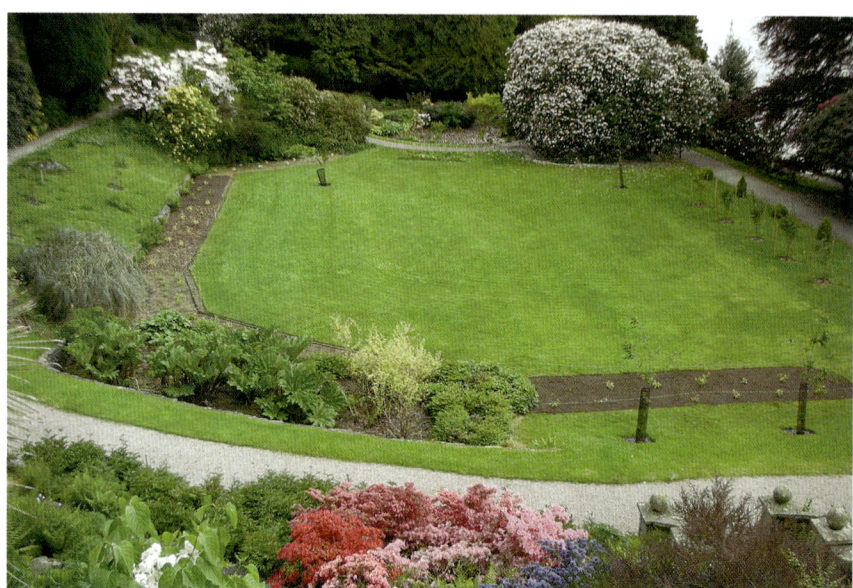

Lower Garden of Langdale Chase from the terrace

Grand Lakeland Mansions

When Cragwood was built using stone quarried from the lake shore, for Mr. Warburton, the front of house terrace gives fantastic views of Windermere and the Lakeland hills. In this garden created by Mawson is a one hundred year old Wisteria, absolutely magnificent in May, which *must* be an original 'Mawson' planting. On the southern side of the house, in May, also, the azaleas and rhododendrons are superb and again at the southern end of the grounds, is a neat and picturesque herb garden,….a chef's delight! A further 'treasure', found in the woodlands of Cragwood, in May, is a hidden Bluebell wood, one of the best in the whole Lake District!

Left: Mawson's majestic stone staircase at Langdale Chase.

Right: Mawson's Bridge at Langdale Chase

Left: One hundred year old Wisteria at Cragwood

Below Right: Terrace at Cragwood

The Life of Thomas Hayton Mawson

Further south on the eastern shore of Windermere was the site chosen for building Moor Crag, a house designed for J.W. Buckley, a wealthy Lancashire mill owner, by Charles Francis Annesley Voysey, an architect who had rapidly risen to fame as one of the leading figures of the Arts and Crafts Movement in this country.

When Voysey showed the house plan to Buckley at Rigg's Hotel, Windermere, on 23rd. June 1899, for approval by him and Mrs Buckley, it was done in the presence of T. H. Mawson, who also signed the document. Thomas Mawson could perhaps have well understood the forthright manner of the younger Charles Voysey, after having listened to a sermon in the past by his father, the Rev. Charles Voysey, who was the last vicar in England to be tried for heresy. The father, however, had many famous friends who respected him and supported him entirely, including the strong-minded author, Eliza Lynn Linton. They soon gathered together to establish him at the Swallow Street Theistic Church in Piccadilly, London. A story that Thomas liked to tell of the younger Voysey was that when a young man, searching for a conversational topic, asked him if he had ever designed anything in a Spanish style, as illustrated in architectural books, Voysey replied, *"I have only one book in my office and that is Bradshaw's Railway Guide which, I am sorry to say, I have to use much oftener than I like."*

Moor Crag.
House designed by
C.F.A. Voysey.
Garden by
T.H. Mawson.

Mawson was engaged to landscape the grounds around Moor Crag which included a long verandah on its southern aspect which Mawson framed with Wisteria. A very taxing part of the plan was to blast through solid rock to create a sweeping, curving uphill driveway from the road to the property.

View from Moor Crag

Entrance drive created through solid rock by Mawson

Chapter 3

THE PRACTICE EXPANDS

Commissions from all over Britain were now coming in and these involved Thomas travelling extensively. So, after the first five years, the Lakeland Nursery and the Landscape Design became two separate businesses, with brothers Robert and Isaac running the Nursery, and Thomas looking for all the garden landscaping work he could find.

In 1900, Thomas designed and built The Corbels for himself and his growing family of six children, so named because of the ornate design of the corbels supporting the guttering to the roof. These beautifully designed corbels were the work of his friend, Dan Gibson. The elder boys attended Windermere Grammar School. At that time, the view from The Corbels covered the whole of the Northern end of Lake Windermere. Robert and his family lived across the road from The Corbels, in one side of a semi-detached house known as Bleak House, also built by the Mawson firm. Sarah, the sister, married Richard Mattocks and they and their four children lived in the other half. Isaac and his wife, Rosa, (nee Bidwell) lived in Oak Street. A semi-detached villa on

The ornate corbels designed by Dan Gibson, on 'The Corbels'

The Corbels Thomas Mawson's home in Windermere

The Practice Expands

Heathwaite was built for other members of the Mawson family. They all worshipped at the Carver United Reform Church in Windermere.

It was at this time that the first edition of Mawson's very large book, "The Art and Craft of Garden-Making" was launched in 1900, having been read over by the Reverend Eric Robertson, Vicar of St. John's Church, Windermere, at the time. Any reader knowing Mr. Robertson as the author of the well-known work, "Wordsworthshire" would know that Thomas had made a very good choice. He also received help in the design from his old friends, Charles E. Mallows, and Dan Gibson.

1901 saw Thomas open a London Office at 28, Conduit Street and, in Bulmers Directory of that year he listed himself as Architect and Surveyor. In Windermere, the Mawson Brothers were listed as Landscape Gardeners-Contracts Undertaken. Shrublands, a very fine house with the round Westmorland chimneys, protruding slated gable, pillared windows and semi-circular rounded centre pane window, (all favoured features of a Mawson designed house) was designed by Thomas for his brother Robert, on New Road, directly opposite the Mawson Nursery. To the side and at the back of Robert's house were plant houses, potting sheds, cool houses, a frame ground, a vinery and an orchard. The property is now known as the Windermere Social Club and unimaginative extensions to the front of the building now hide this part of a once very lovely house. The present car-park to the Social Club was once a tennis lawn belonging to the house.

Mawson on the steps of The Corbels designed for himself and family c.1900

Front Gate to Shrublands

'Shrublands' showing protruding slated gable, half rounded centre window and tennis lawn

Pillared window on Shrublands

Work was now pouring into Mawson's office, after the publication of his book, and old ledgers show that during that year Thomas was engaged on no fewer than thirty garden and town planning schemes. All the brothers were devoted to their work and there was a rare bond of comradeship and affection between them which was strengthened by the fact that the three brothers had married three sisters, or 'as near as'. Thomas and Robert had married the daughters of the late Dr. Edward Prentice, of North Waltham, Anna and Helen, who, upon the death of their father, had been made the wards of their uncle, Mr. Thomas Bidwell, of Trunch, Norfolk, who himself had an only daughter, Rosa. The younger brother, Isaac, had married the latter (Miss Rosa Bidwell) but the three girls always thought of themselves as sisters. It was indeed a particularly happy family and, as they all lived in houses within a short distance of each other, they had daily reunions when at home. Thomas and Robert always admired their younger brother who was full of generous impulses and, yet, showed a wisdom quite beyond his years. He had a great business capacity, was a keen sportsman and a popular employer of labour.

It was therefore a seriously heavy blow which hit the family in 1901. For several days during the month of March, Isaac had had a hard cough but with his usual untiring devotion to business went on with his work, maintaining that he was suffering only from a cold. When matters became worse, he was obliged to consult a doctor who at once put him to bed. The doctor's anxiety showed by making two visits that same night. It was declared to be pneumonia and, although the patient made a great fight for life, at the end of the seventh day he passed away. Not until he had gone, did the family realise the strength and support which Isaac had extended to all.

Chapter 4

NEW YEAR, NEW WORKS

1902 was the year when Mawson's Practice extended to include the planning of Public Parks, housing estates and the re-planning of towns. Mawson's first experience of designing a public park was at Hanley, just outside Stoke-on-Trent, and within six months nearby Burslem Town Council wanted Thomas Mawson to plan a new park for them. These parks, "mostly pick and shovel work" created much needed work for hundreds of men. Thomas reflected in later life that he *"must have been a very young man when he agreed to convert these wastelands of pits, mounds and rubbish tips, under which was buried all the good soil there ever was on the land"* into pleasant public parks.

Photo by permission of W. Brown, Park Manager

Another park design, around this period, was Barrow-in-Furness, where the town was booming. Iron-ore was being transported to the English industrial Midlands, ships were sailing to all corners of the world and the town was a leader in ship-building. The land chosen for the park was 42 acres of farmland with the farmhouse, Piel View Farm, the home of the Slater family, in the centre. The farm was so named because, from there, the distant view of Piel Island with its ruinous Piel Castle could be seen standing at the mouth of the sea-channel leading into the port of Barrow. These buildings, when no longer a farmhouse, eventually were called Piel View House and became the Park offices and home of the resident Park-Keeper. The site was purchased in 1902, but then leased back to the Slater family for the next five years, when work on the park began in 1907/8. Mawson's plans comprised of a bandstand providing a primary focal point, with a huge graduated flight of steps leading up to the highest point of the land. In 1919, a limestone Cenotaph was erected here to honour the local dead of the First World War. Large flower-beds and many recreational facilities such as bowling greens and tennis courts were abundant. The ornamental boating lake was excavated by manual labour which provided much needed work after the First World War. Such land must have been a pleasure to work, after the two afore-mentioned.

*Public Park, Barrow.
Left: Steps descending from Cenotaph to Bandstand.
Right: Bandstand, showing steps ascending.*

Ornamental Shelter beside the Boating Lake, Barrow Public Park.

Mawson was recalled in 1920 to double the size of the boating lake, using two fine bridges in the extension. The second lake had an island in the centre for breeding ducks, geese and water-fowl.

Barrow Park has recently been restored to a very high standard, and the former glory of Mawson's original plans is being created.

One of two bridges Mawson used when doubling the size of the Park Lake, Barrow.

Trees and shrubs beyond the bridge are on the Wildfowl Breeding Island in the extended lake.

1902 saw the Second Edition of "The Art and Craft of Garden Making" published.

In 1904, Mawson had fourteen important new commissions among many smaller ones. About this time, Andrew Carnegie, of Skibo Castle, Dornoch, founded the Carnegie Dunfermline Trust, to which he presented half a million pounds to bring 'sweetness and light' into the lives of the people of his native town, supplemented by the gift of Pittencrieff Park and Glen. The Trust asked Mawson to prepare a scheme for the development of Pittencrieff as a public park. Thomas and his office staff put their heart and soul into months of intensive work on this scheme to improve the city, its parks and surroundings, only to be told, by the *Trustees*, that it was too big and would he modify his plans. When Mawson refused, telling them that this would ruin the whole balance of the scheme, he received not one penny for many months of hard work. Even more hurtful was to think that his efforts would not now contribute to the evolution of Dunfermline.

However, the Dunfermline scheme was to bring him a rich reward eventually, because when Mawson published his report, he won commissions to re-plan many Canadian Towns, and Athens and Salonika in Greece, in time to come.

A short time after this, Mr. Andrew Carnegie invited Thomas to re-plan the gardens at Skibo Castle, in Scotland.

Chapter 5

FAMILY AFFAIRS

Thomas and Anna must have been amongst some of the first (except for the very wealthy) to have a second home. They had a "holiday bungalow" built on the shoreline at Hest Bank, a few miles north of Morecambe, to be of benefit to their eight children who were Edward Prentice (named after his maternal grandfather), John William, Helen Jane, Frances, (known as Frankie) Dorothy, (known as 'Dolly') James Radcliffe (always known as Cliffe), Millicent (known as Mint), and Thomas. A baby girl, May, had died in infancy. This bungalow had many extensions as time went on, the third one being a room to house a full-sized pipe-organ for their frequent 'Musical Evenings'. More and more, Thomas felt that Windermere (though he loved it passionately) was too remote for most of his expanding travelling and, more and more, they lived at the bungalow at Hest Bank. From there, a five-minute walk to the mainline railway station, he could be in London by 1.30pm, whereas from Windermere, it was 4.15pm leaving him less than an hour with his staff at the London office, 28 Conduit Street. From the very first opening of the London office, Thomas had placed in charge James Crossland, his first pupil who was still with the firm. During his time there, Mr. Crossland became as well known to the clients as Mawson himself. He was a hard worker and, like all the staff, most loyal to the interests of the firm.

One thing missing for the family, in Hest Bank, was a suitable church in which to worship, as they had been regular attenders at the Carver United Reform Church, in Windermere. The architect, Dan Gibson, was asked to design a small Congregational Chapel and Mawson was very much involved in the interior adornment. Later, it would seem that Thomas re-designed the

Mawson's Bungalow on the shoreline at Hest Bank, extended to three times its original size

entrance porch, putting the door on the southern aspect where the prevailing westerly rain would not drive in. The inside of the new porch had all the design details favoured by Thomas including a pillared window with round topped centre pane. He designed a carved, folding screen which, when drawn across, enclosed a smaller space for the greater comfort of the sparse winter congregation. This was to be made by Simpsons of Kendal, who were a well respected firm of craftsmen in wood established by A.W. Simpson in 1881. Thomas gave much thought as to the funding for such a fine screen and it occurred to him to ask for donations from members of Parliament he felt he knew sufficiently well to approach. He succeeded admirably up to the last panel and, as a last hope, he wrote to Mr. Lever, of "Sunlight Soap" fame,

Congregational Chapel at Hest Bank

Dan Gibson's design for the chapel

The chapel with porch entrance changed by T.H. Mawson designed with interior window pillars and rounded central window.

whom he had never met but knew that he was a fellow High Church Nonconformist also. Mr. Lever's reply was characteristic and revealed the humour and generosity for which he was known. The letter which came from Thornton Manor contained a cheque for the remaining cost of the carved panel screen. Lever wished Mawson every success.

The next feature was the central pulpit, also carved by the well-known craftsman, Mr. A.W. Simpson, of Kendal, to whose generosity the Church is indebted for the beautiful hymn board. The charming pulpit fall with lilies in white silk appliqué and green silk on a crimson and old gold ground, was the work and gift of Mrs. A. W. Simpson and the Bible cushion from which it falls was the work and gift of Mrs. Milner. The communion table was the gift of the architect, Dan Gibson. (The last panel of the screen was not completed until 1905.) These details, published by 'The Bazaar Committee of the Hest-Bank Congregational Church', shows how very proud of their little church the residents were.

The carved wooden, folding screen was the outstanding feature of the little church and the one of which the congregation were most proud. It was financed entirely by the following politicians :- Colonel Sandys, MP., George White, Esq. MP., William Hesketh Lever, Esq.,MP., and Norval W. Helme, Esq., MP.

Thomas then had ideas for creating a model village at Hest Bank. He designed houses behind the chapel in Lonsdale Road and on the main road, Marine Drive, in particular, a lovely house with six high pillars on its front elevation and called The Pillars.

Thomas was now averaging 20,000 miles a year in travel, mostly on trains on which he always carried a portable drawing case, to carry on working as he travelled. As a point of interest to Lakeland folk, Thomas recorded: *"The late Arthur Simpson, craftsman, of Kendal, made for me a handy and portable drawing-case with a fold-over lid, large enough to take half an Imperial sheet of drawing paper. When closed, the case contained my mathematical instruments, scales, and small set-squares"*.

Thomas Mawson with his
'Simpson' made
Portable Drawing Case
Photograph by kind permission of Mr. T.P. Mawson.

Chapter 6

THE GOLDEN YEARS

The years of 1905-06 were the most momentous of Mawson's career, for it was during that time that his long connection and friendship with William Hesketh Lever began, after Lever had made his contribution to the little church in Hest Bank.

Thomas received a letter from W. H. Lever, containing not only the cheque for the full cost of the remaining panel of the wooden screen inside the Congregational church at Hest Bank, but also an invitation to improve the garden at Thornton Manor, a residence in the Elizabethan style, which was one of Mr. Lever's homes near Port Sunlight. This was an unexpected reward to Thomas for his interest in the church and certainly not anticipated.

Mr. Lever's letter had read; *"Now that you have had the courage to ask me for a subscription, may I be so bold as to ask you to come and advise me upon the improvement of my garden at Thornton Manor? I have wanted to consult you for the last two years, but all my friends warned me that it would be useless, as you never worked for anyone holding less social rank than a Duke, whereas I am only a poor indigent soap-maker. Let me know if you can come, and when.*

Yours Faithfully, William Hesketh Lever.

They fixed a convenient date to meet and it was arranged that Mawson should stay two days at Thornton Manor. Mr. Lever received Thomas with a smile and a hearty handshake, which put Thomas at his ease at once.

William Hesketh Lever, Thomas quickly realised, was a man of strong personality, who had absolute control of himself and all his interests, which also included his few leisure hours. After evening dinner, the two men walked backwards and forwards in the garden discussing many subjects. On parting for the night, Mr. Lever had said, with a twinkle in his eye, *"I shall be out in the garden at a quarter past six in the morning; I hope this is not too early for you. I can give you an hour and a quarter and we breakfast at half-past seven"*. Thomas agreed that this was quite convenient. Prompt to the time, Mr. Lever was there in riding attire, having just returned from the morning canter which he always enjoyed after going through his private correspondence. Thomas began to wonder how many hours sleep he thought necessary. Needless to say, Lever outlined a formal garden of heroic proportions! This was the first taste of Lever's strong personality, but they were like-minded men and remained firm friends through many, many commissions. Thomas created flower-decked walkways at Thornton Manor for Lever to pace up and down whilst thinking or talking, as he liked to do.

Very soon after this first meeting, Lever was swept into Parliament as a Liberal candidate in the great 'landslide' election of 1906. He was rather surprised and not at all elated at having to face life in Westminster. It brings a smile to relate that having got to the House of Commons, Lever put forward a plan for its reconstruction. He proposed to improve the appearance of the Palace of Westminster by rebuilding the Terrace of the House of Commons so that it had two tiers. The Ministry of Works did not proceed with the plan.

Left: One of the two Saxon barns at Rivington

Right: The tithe barn type interior 'A pleasure to behold'

Mawson's next momentous task for Lever was to landscape 400 acres of Rivington Pike into a park and leisure area, to be given to the people of Bolton by Lever. To start, about twenty miles of good metalled roads were constructed to replace the former moorland tracks.

After providing the access, the problem of providing shelter for the people was solved very easily, as there were, described by Thomas as, *"two immense Saxon barns, picturesque externally, and with internal roof construction of the tithe-barn type, a pleasure to behold"*, which had previously been put into a good state of repair by Mr. Lever's local architect, Mr. Jonathan Simpson. (Lever and Simpson had started school together in Miss Aspinwall's class where they were the closest of friends, and remained so all their lives) A short distance away was a well-proportioned mansion of the former squires of the estate, known as Rivington Hall, which had been converted into a Picture Gallery and Art Museum. Of interest were the paddocks around the Hall, stocked with zebras, deer, buffaloes, emus, wallabies, yak and even a lioness cub. The lake in front of the Hall was divided into two with one lake housing white swans and the other black swans, from Australia. These things existed in 1904, before Mawson started work on the Pike.

Landscaping fifty acres of the Pike, around Roynton Cottage (midway up the Pike) for Leverhulme's private use, was no easy task. This was the second building on this site, the first being called merely The Bungalow and of wooden construction which was burnt down by suffragette Edith Rigby, of Winkley Square, Preston, who admitted the arson attack. Lever immediately re-built his 'cottage' in stone, sympathetically constructed to conform to the ancient Lancashire traditions and given a flat roof of reinforced concrete to

The Golden Years

deter any further arson attacks. He named the building 'Roynton Cottage'. This was to be very grand for entertaining his guests and, some time later, a Ballroom was added as William Lever became very fond of dancing. As an example of the attention Lever paid to every detail of his home, where ever he lived, in the ballroom, at Roynton Cottage, a glass dome in the centre of the circular ceiling gave light whilst the rest was decorated in deep blue and dotted with gold stars which were arranged as the constellations appeared on the 19th September 1851, the date of Lever's birth. To put his mountain home into appropriate surroundings Lever, always used to the best, could think of no man more able than Thomas Mawson, with his futuristic vision. On this Mawson mused many years later; *"The new house bespoke a garden in keeping with it, and of all the gardens which have ministered to my professional enjoyment, none comes into competition with Roynton. The reason is a very human one. Everyone prophesied failure. All pointed to the tufts of bent and mountain fescue, the only growth to be found on the mountainside, and laughed at the notion of anything else growing. Undismayed by the pessimists, we laid out our nurseries and planted thousands of rhododendrons, including choice hybrids and many interesting species of Alpine varieties."*

*Below Left:
Roynton Cottage above the Great Lawn, showing the rocky outcrop, far left*

*Below Right:
Mrs. E.P. Mawson and Mrs T.H. Mawson on the veranda at Roynton Cottage*

The whole of the land in question lay on the western slopes of Rivington Pike, which rises to about 1,200 feet above sea level, reaching down to a chain of artificial lakes almost three miles long which supply Liverpool with water, his own private residence being on the higher slopes of the pike, leaving the crest free to the public. The gardens to Roynton Cottage and

Left: Part of Japanese Garden at 'Roynton Cottage'.

Right: Part of Japanese Garden and lake. The lantern contained a small lamp.

Rivington Park were parts of one commission and were to be laid out in perfect keeping with their natural environment. Over the next twenty years, on this bleak hillside, Mawson created a Japanese Garden, an Italian Garden and The Mountain Garden, all planted with hardy species from his Lakeland Nursery, which became respected nationwide. In order to overcome the sloping angle of descent, the gardens, lawns and a Bowling Green were laid out in terraces, which meant flattening large areas of hillside. On the great lawn below the Bungalow, a large rocky outcrop about seven feet high was left as a feature to show how much material was removed to construct a flat lawn.

It is reputed that Lever showed Mawson a blue and white Willow Pattern plate saying he'd quite like something like that at the southern end of the garden. He asked Thomas if he could incorporate something similar? The resulting Japanese Garden was spectacular! The red sandstone cliffs uncovered by the excavation made a perfect site for waterfalls cascading from the Pike above into a large lake, complete with a flock of flamingoes. Three wooden pagodas were placed around the lake and used as tea houses, and a large stone lantern containing a small lamp stood on a pedestal in the lake and made an attractive feature.

West of the Japanese Garden was the Mountain Garden and Mawson used a style that he had used worldwide. Mostly he had introduced water from mountain streams and at Rivington there was no shortage of water from the moor above. He designed a constructed gorge of artificial rock outcrops

The Golden Years

and a series of pools where the path was made to meander and cross the stream by way of two stone bridges. The end result was a woodland walk through a 'ravine'. The Italian Garden at Rivington could never be truly Italian, of course, as the species planted had to be able to survive the Lancashire winters, but the building style was that of the Roman era, and featured more a network of footpaths, loggias and summerhouses giving seven different viewpoints, one being a vista across the Lancashire plain to the Cumbrian mountains, on a clear day. The main feature, the idea coming entirely from Lord Leverhulme, was a spectacular Romanesque style, seven-arched bridge to cross Roynton Lane. When Lever told his stonemason he wanted a seven-arched bridge the mason said it couldn't be done. Lever wasted no more time on the subject. He said to the man, *"Pack a suitcase, I'm going to show you what I want!* The next morning they flew off to Lagos, Nigeria, where Leverhulme owned a plantation. Whilst there, Lever took him to see a magnificent seven-arched bridge, *"There,"* he said, *"that's what I want"*. He got his seven-arched bridge! By 1920, Lever had a workforce of 100 men employed on the construction of Mawson's plans.

The terraced Gardens of Rivington was one of the finest examples of Mawson's Mountain Garden style of design for which he gained a world wide reputation. Another commission was the designing of Leverhulme's house gardens at "The Hill", in Hampstead.

Leverhulme's Romanesque seven arched bridge, from a design near his plantation in Nigeria.

The bridge crosses a road on Rivington Pike.

Chapter 7

LIGHT AND SHADOW ALONG THE WAY

Leverhulme's house known as 'The Hill' in Hampstead

In 1906 Mawson was commissioned to improve and extend the garden at Duffryn House, near Swansea, in the Vale of Glamorgan, South Wales, by wealthy owner, Reginald Cory, a keen amateur horticulturist.

Pompeiian Garden at Duffryn House

The plan followed all the elements for which Mawson gardens became known; formality near the house with terraces, lawns and flower beds, progressing through the more intimate and less formal areas further from the house. Irish yews were used for formality close to the house, as were

Light and Shadow Along the Way

Mawson's favoured balustraded terraces. The garden merged into the surrounding countryside on its boundaries. There was also a Pompeiian Garden from which annual flowers were planted and allowed to hang in festoons from the tops of the colonnades and roof of the loggia, in summer. There was a central raised pool and fountain. The splendour of Mawson's great lawn was enhanced by a central water-lily canal that held Mr. Cory's collection of *Nymphaea*.

"Lindeth Fell", built on ground high above Bowness-on-Windermere in 1907, is another example of a superb Country House where Mawson excelled in making the garden seem to wrap itself round the house as if they were one. A clever creation of a large lake, on the other side of the sweeping driveway, gave occasion for the gentle pleasure of boating and perhaps it may have been stocked with fish. At this time, "The Art & Craft of Garden Making" was going into its third edition.

Below: Lindeth Fell, Windermere, Cumbria

Left: Under the clematis arch to the second terrace

Right: The lake at Lindeth Fell, Windermere

The Life of Thomas Hayton Mawson

2nd Terrace level, The Lavender Border, Lindeth Fell

Clematis Montana at Lindeth Fell Windermere

Tragically, on 19th June 1907, the architect Dan Gibson died, too young at an age of only forty one years. There remain many intricate designs attributed to Gibson in wrought iron, slate, stone and wood in the Lake District. He was working on the beautiful wrought iron gates at Graythwaite Hall when he first met Thomas Mawson. Their friendship matured into a working partnership over the next two years. It was the combination of Mawson and Gibson that produced work like Brockhole, White Craggs at

Clappersgate and Dawstone, now in part called Heathwaite Manor, Windermere. Gibson had come to the Lake District from Lincolnshire as a young man of twenty four years, anxious to gain practical experience as an architect, but then seemed to prefer designing smaller decorative works. He is remembered in Windermere for designing the memorial gates to Dr. Archibald Hamilton at Queen's Park. Unfortunately, in the 1940's Dan Gibson's gates went the way of so many other wrought-iron works of art, to be melted down to make weapons for the Second World War . If they had survived they would doubtlessly now be listed as of architectural and historical importance. An exact replica now replaces them.

There is more of Gibson's fine work to be found in the Lake District in the form of sundials, weather-vanes and ornamental statues made to his specification by local craftsmen. Gibson and Mawson often visited Arthur Simpson, the master wood-carver, at his cottage The Homestead at Ghyll Head, Windermere, where he held summer school style carving classes. Through the liaison of these talented men came perhaps one of Gibson's most intricate designs. It was a very fine Rood screen designed for St. John's Church, Windermere. Under Simpson's guidance, the vicar of St. John's at this time Eric Robertson, holding the locum tenency, carved the central panel of five and the six foot high cross on top of the screen, and parishioners the other four. This intricately designed wooden screen is now in St. Martin's Church, Bowness-on-Windermere, as part of the vestry.

When Dan Gibson lost his fight for life, Thomas Mawson wrote 'An Appreciation' of his life in the Architectural Association Journal in August of that year. In it he said that it was eighteen years since he had first met Dan Gibson, then a handsome, manly young fellow, charming in manner, with a keen appreciation of the beautiful. He was abounding with industry and genius for architecture and all kinds of craftsmanship. He had a most happy faculty of firing everyone with his own enthusiasm. During their brief partnership, Mawson had had the opportunity of watching Gibson's development that led to that perfect mastery of design. In addition, Dan Gibson had a wide knowledge of furniture, silver and jewellery. Even those who counted him as a friend had little idea of the amount and variety the work he was designing. Architecturally, he had designed Dawstone for Mr. A. M. Synge, 1903/4, three years after designing Brockhole.

At the time of his death he had commenced designing a large new residence in Winster, near Windermere, for Higgin Birkett esq. Today this lovely house is known as Birkett Houses.

Mawson's tribute to Dan Gibson was, *"Gibson was one of the handsomest, most courtly, and able men I have ever known."* His death was a great loss to the community.

Chapter 8

A FRIENDSHIP LEADS TO AMERICA

Work on plans in several locations was progressing well for Mawson, when he was visited by an American gentleman, Mr. Theodore Marburg from Baltimore, later America's ambassador to Paris. During Mr. Marburg's prolonged stay in England, Mawson spent occasional evenings visiting Mr. Marburg at his hired mansion in Windermere. Several years before, Thomas had landscaped the garden where they

> "spent lovely summer evenings watching the glorious sight of glowing sunsets dipping down behind the majestic barrier of mountains at the head of Windermere , during which we were awed to silence. The spell which others than poets have felt in this district, was upon us."

The two men had so much in common that, upon the eventual departure of Mr. Marburg for America, Thomas felt *'a distinct sense of loss.'* However, very soon afterwards, a letter arrived from Mr. Marburg telling Thomas of some young friend of his, the direct heir to one of their colonial mansions and estates, situated at Green Spring Valley, Massachusetts, who was keen to consult Mr. Mawson about his garden. The thought of seeing this part of the United States filled Thomas with pleasure, especially as he had been studying civic design and had written essays upon the subject, which he was later to incorporate into a book. His eldest son, Edward Prentice, on hearing the news and having just completed his second year at the London School of Architecture, caught his father's enthusiasm and persuaded him that he would be essential to his father's success.

During the eight-day trip aboard the 'Cedric', father and son made many friends who helped in many ways on later trips to America. It was the end of September. Their train journey of twenty-five miles to their destination enabled them to see the glorious countryside of that area known as part of "New England". They noted the abundant copses of native trees and shrubs, which were deeply interesting to them, with little farmsteads interspersed, and timber-built churches of the colonial neo-classic design. They arrived at their destination, the mansion known as "Brooklandwood", in Green Spring Valley, and stayed for three weeks surveying, contouring and planning the whole garden scheme and completing it in approved draft form to take back home to prepare the working drawings and details. As the Browns were collectors of Chippendale and Sheraton furniture, they visited London again in spring of the next year. Mawson asked Mr. Lever's permission to show them his collection of paintings and furniture, which was readily granted. On completing the tour, Mr. Brown remarked, with good humour; *"I can only suggest that, for completion, Mr. Lever should panel his doors with Romneys"*.

Early in 1908, the Mawson Business established a main office at No. 2 High Street, Lancaster, or simply, 'High Street House' as it was known, and the firm was to remain there for twenty-eight years, having a staff of between

A Friendship Leads to America

twenty-five and thirty people. It was very spacious and central in the British Isles. An interesting addition to the staff came at this time and gave a story that Thomas was fond of relating in later years. The new young man's name was Howard Grubb. In 1907, he had written to Mr. Mawson from his home in the U.S.A., saying that he very much wished to come and work in the Mawson office. He had trained at the School of Landscape Architecture at the Cornell University, in U.S.A. Thomas had replied thanking him at the time and advising him not to leave America, as he was sure there would be more openings for him there than here, in Britain. The letter was forgotten. Now here he was, a fine, upstanding young fellow, with a good build, saying, *"My name is Grubb, and I have come to work for you!"* Thomas, taken aback, replied that he was sorry, but every seat in his office was full, but Grubb continued, *"Well, sir, I have worked my way from America on a cattle boat, so that I might have the honour of working for you, so you must find me a seat somewhere."* What could Thomas do with determination like this? Howard Grubb got his seat. Late one afternoon, when Grubb was working late in the office, Thomas remembered that he was to give a vote of thanks to a Miss Dunnington who was lecturing on garden design to members of the Architectural Association. To reward Grubb for his work, Thomas offered to take him along. He introduced him to Miss Dunnington and, three months later, was told of their engagement. They married and the firm of Dunnington-Grubb became a leading firm of landscape architects, in Canada. At this point Thomas had already written two editions of his very large and popular book, "The Art and Craft of Garden Making". There were to be five editions in total. Also by July of that year, Thomas had no fewer than twenty substantial new commissions. 1908 was such an action-packed year that the output was more than any other two years combined.

Mawson's office No. 2 High Street, Lancaster known as High Street House.

Chapter 9

MORE TRAVEL ABROAD

Perhaps the crowning commission of this important year was when Thomas was invited to accept an appointment as the British representative in the limited international competition to plan the gardens surrounding the Palace of Peace at The Hague. This was an experience which aroused his greatest enthusiasm and he was very quickly on his way to The Hague, accompanied by his eldest son, Edward Prentice. Introducing themselves to the British Ambassador, Sir Henry Howard, who received them with every kindness, they were instantly aware that the old sportsman was really anxious for his countrymen to win. The next morning, they made their way to the Buiterust Palace, the site of the Palace of Peace and there met the resident architect, Mr. Van de Steur. Thomas and his son began at once on their survey of all the old trees on the site. This took about a week. Then they returned home to complete their designs within the time allowed. This scheme included not only the layout of the gardens and terraces, but also a little town planning in the avenue opposite the main entrance. Mawson's scheme was duly despatched and, on 20th July 1908, Thomas received a letter of congratulations from Sir Henry Howard announcing that he had won the Competition and that other entries were 'immeasurably inferior' to his own. The gardens were completed in 1913, with much of the work on the ground being in charge of Edward Prentice Mawson in its early stages. Later it was in the hands of Mawson's Quaker pupil, Mr. Howard Grubb, and was finally completed with Mr. Norman Dixon in charge. The opening of the Peace Palace was a magnificent function, performed by the Queen of the Netherlands in the presence of many distinguished personages and foreign ambassadors.

'The Palace of Peace' The Hague.

The Palace of Peace where Mawson landscaped the surrounding gardens.

Back in his home-base of Lancaster, Mawson was commissioned to extend the gardens at "Bailrigg", Scotforth, now the Medical Centre for Lancaster University, but then, c.1908, the principal home of Herbert Lushington Storey, J.P., D.L. Herbert was one of the most generous sons of his father, Sir Thomas Storey, whose public spirit was to be of great importance to Thomas a few years later. All that was required at this time was to landscape the west side of the grounds which sloped down in a mighty sweep, giving views of Morcambe Bay and the mountains of the Lake District. On the north, south and east sides of the house, the gardens had been adequately laid out by Mr. Ernest Milner. Unfortunately, nearly all Mawson's work has since disappeared to become sports fields for the University. Only one wall of the west side, built to accommodate alpine plants, can now be seen, screening the small formal garden around the house.

1909 saw Mawson appointed to a lectureship in Landscape Design at the University of Liverpool School of Civic Art.

'Bailrigg' the home of Herbert Lushington Storey at the beginning of the 20th century. Now the Medical Centre for Lancaster University.

Chapter 10

WELCOME RETURN TO THE LAKE DISTRICT

Rydal Hall, Rydal, Cumbria.

Grounds landscaped by Thomas Mawson in 1909.

Working in his beloved Lake District again, Mawson was called to landscape the grounds at the front of Rydal Hall into a formal garden for Stanley Hughes Le Fleming. On the estate and close to Rydal Hall was "Rydal Mount", the house in which William Wordsworth was a tenant from 1813 until his death in 1850. He had roamed this area frequently for all the thirty-

Formal Garden in front of 'Rydal Hall', with pond and ornamental fountain.

seven years that he lived there. Rydal Hall would have been similar, in commission, to Graythwaite Hall, giving Mawson the space and opportunity to incorporate terraces with lots of balustrading and steps, from the right and from the left, leading to a central, circular pond with a statuary fountain of a boy holding a spouting fish. Placed around the formal rectangular garden were bench seats with double pillars at either end to support a pergola for

The Lower Rydal Falls, with the Grot House viewing Station lower left.

The Lower Rydal Falls, as viewed in a 'picture frame' from the Grot House.

climbing, flowering plants. In between the seats were herbaceous borders and, on the lawn, clipped box hedging surrounded geometrical flowerbeds. On the southern side of the formal garden, further steps led down to a grotto and a lower level path. On the eastern end of the garden, steps leading down to the croquet lawn were decorated with a statue of a lion on either side. This was the first occasion in which Mawson had been persuaded to use cement in making the garden statuary and, now almost a hundred years later, this cement work is crumbling and a massive restoration of the garden is at present being undertaken. From the croquet lawn, through a small gate, a path leads down to the Grot House (or summer house). This very small stone building is marked on plans dated 1668. Upon entering, one is faced with the best possible view of the Lower Rydal Falls through a four feet square opening in the wall, which frames the Falls like a frame on a picture. We are told that this is the way folk liked to view the wild scenery in those very early years, as they were a little afraid of the 'wilderness' uncontained, and this little 'Grot House' (Grot meaning as in 'Dell') is probably one of the very first buildings built as a viewing 'Station' in the whole of the country, and is important architecturally and historically. No work by Mawson was needed here; it could not be improved upon. The bridge which crosses Rydal Beck close to the Grot House has a very cleverly built tunnel running along the bank underneath.

Within a few miles south of Rydal Hall, the Mawson firm was commissioned to landscape the grounds of the beautiful mansion known as Briery Close, in 1910. It was here that the author, Charlotte Bronte, had stayed for a few weeks as the guest of Sir James Kay-Shuttleworth, in August, 1850. From 'The Briery', as the mansion was then known, Charlotte wrote with eloquence to her friend, Miss Wooler, on 27th. September, 1850, of her

The wonderful view beyond the Great Lawn from Briery Close.

Welcome Return to the Lake District

Azealea, maple & rhododendron in a Mawson garden at Briery Close Windermere.

host; *"He very kindly showed me the scenery, 'as can be seen from a carriage'..and I discerned that the 'Lake Country' is a glorious region, of which I had only seen the similitude in dream…waking or sleeping. ….I longed to slip out unseen, and to run away by myself in amongst the hills and dales. Erratic and vagrant instincts tormented me, and these I was obliged to control, or rather suppress, for fear of*

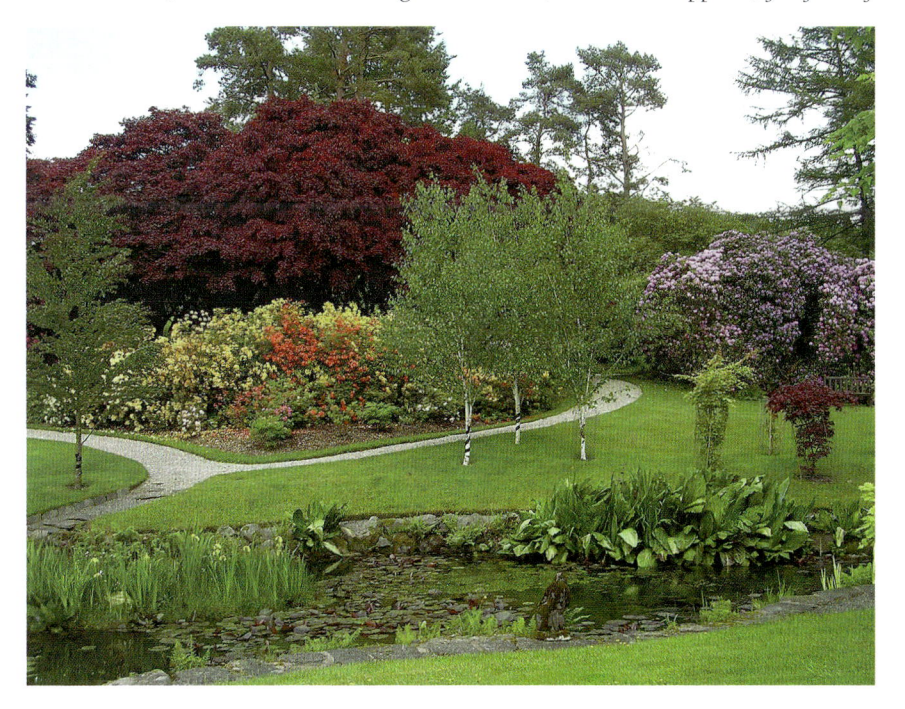

The beautiful garden at Briery Close Windermere.

The Life of Thomas Hayton Mawson

growing in any degree enthusiastic, and thus drawing attention to myself." Terraces and lawns at the front of the mansion provide a panoramic view of the breathtaking scene of lake and mountains laid before one. Little wonder that Charlotte was over-whelmed by the scene she beheld!

Commissions for Mr. Lever were always growing in number, interest and importance, and now included gardens and terraces to Hall-i-th'-Wood, Bolton, Lancashire, one of the most famous examples of half-timbered mansions in the country. Built in the fifteenth century, it had been bought by W. H. Lever, c. 1909, thoroughly and reverently repaired and restored by Mr. Lever's architects, furnished in keeping with its period, and presented to his native town of Bolton. Guided tours of the house demonstrate a double four-poster bed where, under the mattress filled with straw, was one continuous rope threaded forwards and backwards across the base. When the rope sagged with use, it could be pulled and tightened again. This, say the guides, was the original meaning of the saying, "Goodnight, sleep tight!". Thomas would have been well aware that it was here in this house that Samuel Crompton had invented his Spinning Mule, in 1779. Here also, on the vast stretches of moorland which gave Bolton its old name of Bolton-le-Moors, Mawson had performed the mammoth commission of landscaping Rivington Pike, (also given to the people of Bolton), for Mr. Lever.

Part of the lake in the lawn at Briery Close

Hall-i-th'-Wood, Bolton.

Thomas was now covering commissions all over Britain and travelling thousands of miles by train, on which he continued his writing and drawing. Never a minute was wasted.

When working for Mrs. Gordon Canning of Hartpury House, about three miles from Gloucester, Thomas was planning an extension to the gardens plus additional tennis lawns and herbaceous borders, while practically all the walls were utilised for alpine plants. The beautiful wrought-iron garden gate was the work of Mrs. Ames Lyde, the lady blacksmith of Thornham, Norfolk, from designs by Edward Prentice Mawson. Thomas had first been introduced to Mrs. Lyde in Florence, where she had a palace with a beautiful garden, at which she spent half the year. The other half was spent on her Norfolk estate, mostly in her blacksmith's shop, where she trained village lads in the craft of the smith, which was becoming a thriving village industry. When Thomas had met Mrs Lyde for the first time, in Florence, he had commented on the various pieces of intricate Italianate ironwork on the garden walls, the garden gates and grilles of superb design and workmanship, the wrought-iron fencing and a host of other such work. She was amused, *"Don't you know I am the lady blacksmith?"* she had asked. Much to his embarrassment, Thomas admitted that he had no such knowledge. Later, Thomas commissioned her to do considerable work for him, of which the gates at Hartpury House in Gloucester, were one of them. It was an experience and a delight to see her in her workshop, or to spend an hour in her company discussing roses, which she grew to perfection.

This was followed by a most important public work for the Southport Corporation for which he redesigned the Lord Street Gardens, the Marine Lake, Park and Promenade. Lord Street Boulevard, with its sunken gardens, is universally admired.

Any spare moments Thomas spent in writing books. Between 1900 and 1926, he had written sixteen books or pamphlets.

Gates at Hartpury House for Mrs Gordon Canning.

Made by Mrs Ames Lyde, lady blacksmith.

Chapter 11

THE HISTORY OF WOOD HALL

A difficult and demanding project, in 1910, was Wood Hall, near Cockermouth, where Mawson landscaped a very steep bank into a superbly grand garden, surrounding the old house.

The history known of this area is truly amazing and is safely in the hands of the present owners. It is first mentioned in the year 849 when it belonged to the Monastery of Guisborough. Much later, in 1535, the land was owned by King Henry V111, who sold it to "Henry Tolson-Gentleman" for £337-16 shillings and 8 pence. Mr. Tolson then built the house at the foot of the bank, which became Wood Hall. The artist, J. M. W. Turner, loved the view from here and selected it as the subject for two of his paintings in the 1770's. The Victorian Gothic Mansion was built at the base of the very steep bank around

The old Wood Hall a Victorian Gothic Mansion, demolished in c.1949.

Below left: Steps leading to the upper garden and summer house.

Below right: The double summer house on the middle terrace.

46

The History of 'Wood Hall'

1870 and it was the five acres of grounds around this house that Mawson was invited to landscape in 1910. A workforce of forty craftsmen were employed. The garden was magnificent when completed and many photographs of such a fine piece of work are displayed in Mawson's 'The Art & Craft of Garden Making' book of 1912. The entrance was by a carriageway across parkland turning into a sweeping driveway which ended in a carriage turning circle at the front of the house. From the balustraded, semi-circular terrace, a double stone stairway went down into woodland walks. Beyond the house was a beautiful, stone pillared, rose covered pergola. There were three summerhouses, one being of double size, and one of triple size with the interiors panelled in oak. Unfortunately, during World War 2, when most of the men were away serving their country, the garden became heavily overgrown and the mansion was demolished in about 1949 due to an unknown seepage of water rotting the timbers and much of the stone was sold off. The stone outline of the old house still remains in the lower lawn as a thoughtful reminder of the site of the house now belonging to history. The new, elevated Wood Hall was built by converting the old barn (built 1821) and stables, on the highest point of the land, into a beautiful house in 1970. Thomas Mawson's garden has been patiently resurrected over the past thirty-five years by the hard work, love and devotion of the present owners.

New, elevated Wood Hall, built 1970.

Thoughtfully, the base of the old Wood Hall remains as a very helpful feature.

In the summer of 1910 Thomas and his wife joined an organised tour of the continent to view Housing and Town Planning. Their first visit was to Salzburg where Thomas was impressed by the perfection of the town gardening. Next stop was Vienna, a city of great beauty and cleanliness, where they attended a sumptuous dinner on the evening of their arrival. It was an impressive example of perfect organisation. Had the dinner been a part of a great military pageant, it could not have been carried out with greater precision.

The original triple Summer House at Wood Hall near Cockermouth

The conference, after that, went without a hitch and goodwill was obtained on all sides. The study of Vienna, with its wonderful avenues and gardens and its splendid buildings, did much to enlarge the vision of the visiting town planners.

On the return journey, they spent a week-end in Dresden and Thomas was to write, *"I have never seen another city that impressed me so much,......Dresden will ever remain in my memory as a lovable city of sweet smelling lilacs."* Finally, they made a visit to Berlin, travelling home via Hamburg.

On his return, after three weeks away, there was a letter from Mr. Samuel (now Lord) Waring, telling Thomas he had recommended him to replan the Royal gardens of Queen Alexandra at her home, 'Hvidore', Copenhagen. Lord Waring was head of the highly respected firm of furniture-making, Waring and Gillow of Lancaster, for whom Thomas had prepared, in the past, an extensive garden scheme at his home, Foots Cray Place, Kent. From that time onwards, they had become firm friends, hence the introduction for Thomas to Queen Alexandra, by Lord Waring. This necessitated a visit to the Danish capital. Arriving at 'Hvidore', a residence of moderate size, the plot to be remodelled was of some two acres in extent. The site was windy from the seaward side as the stunted and leaning trees denoted. The plan was to divide one garden into three simple lateral parts, each having a long herbaceous border with climbing roses on trellis fencing for protection against the wind. The existing walls were hidden with a profusion of interesting climbing plants and flowers. The whole when finished was just a snug floral paradise. A year later, Mawson's son Edward Prentice Mawson designed a two storey tower to overlook this garden and command the views seaward.

Chapter 12

LECTURING IN THE USA AND CANADA

'The Art and Craft of Garden Making' book had met with a ready sale in America, and this led to correspondents in all departments of horticulture and architecture. This wide correspondence gradually crystallised into an invitation to take up a lecture tour in America. For months, every spare moment was devoted to the preparation of his forthcoming lectures. The slide photography was very ably undertaken by Mr. James Crossland, Thomas's secretary and manager.

His lectures were on 'Landscape Architecture' and 'Civic Art'.

Thomas Mawson left Liverpool on 26th September, 1910 by White Star Line, on s.s.Celtic heading for New York to undertake his first American Lecture Tour. During the voyage he became acquainted with a lady at the dinner table whom he found to be Mrs. Finch, one of America's best known educationists and a barrister-at-law. On this and succeeding visits to America, Mawson always lectured at the school organised and established by her. His next lecture was delivered before the School of Landscape Architecture at Cornell University. From there he returned to New York where he gave three lectures before the School of Architecture at Columbia University. The next engagement was in the historic old town of Richmond, Virginia, which meant three days of travelling, and this for one lecture only. However the society engaging him paid all his expenses in addition to his fee. His subject was "The Charm of the English Garden".

Returning to New York, he lectured to a large audience on "Garden Villages in England", quoting Lord Leverhulme's Port Sunlight as the most successful example so far realised in any part of the world. This statement was met with a suggestion of resentment that Thomas had ignored certain experiments in industrial housing then being made in America.

Whilst lecturing in Philadelphia, Thomas was invited to the home of Graham Bell, of telephone fame, whom he had met on board the "Celtic". Accepting the invitation, Thomas travelled to Washington and was escorted to his home. He found that Mr. Bell had arranged for him to give a lecture in his great parlour on the day of his arrival. Seldom had Thomas met so distinguished a company. Being slightly nervous, he was advised by Mr. Bell to discard his manuscript and just give a simple account of the housing movement in England. He did, and was heartily congratulated by all.

The next day Thomas was shown round the capital, confirming his previous impression that Washington was potentially the most beautiful capital in the world.

From Washington he returned to New York, then on to Chicago. At a luncheon he gave an address on "The Town Planning Movement in Europe". For once, Thomas frankly acknowledged that our continent had nothing so ambitious as Daniel Burnam's scheme for the reorganisation of Chicago, in fact he felt that in many ways Chicago was pointing the way to other cities and to other countries.

The next morning, Thomas met Daniel Burnam. Burnam was a big man, with all the simplicity and modesty of those truly great. For two hours they talked, about Thomas's work, and about Burnam's work, and in particular, their great hopes for the future. Looking back on his life's work, and looking forward to his end, of which Burnam had confided in Mawson, he had already had a warning, he said, *"Whatever happens, I feel that I have done a day's work, and there is great satisfaction in that."* Burnam's great services were one of the most remarkable examples in America of that spirit which was creating a new sense of civic responsibility.

Mawson undertook several commissions in Canada, including drawing plans for the development of the Canadian National Park at Niagara Falls. These were never fulfilled. The Niagara Falls Park Commission decided that their funds could not afford professional advice. Although work on these plans proved to be a waste of Mawson's valuable time, the trip was successful in other respects.

Sir Robert Borden, who had spoken on Mawson's behalf in the 'Niagara Falls Park Commission', did what he could to atone for Mawson's disappointment by recommending that Thomas be selected to replan Banff in the Rockies, including a large section of the great national park there. The goodwill shown to Mawson by the Premier was of great assistance in securing introductions and requests for lectures on city planning from a dozen important centres, beginning with Ottawa and including Montreal, Halifax (Nova Scotia), St. John (New Brunswick), St. Marie Port Arthur, Winnipeg, Regina, Saskatoon, Medicine Hat, Calgary, Vancouver, and Victoria (B.C.). He gave a series of lectures on the necessity for Town Planning legislation in Canada. In months of work, *"his days were spent with clients and his nights in railway journeys".*

Thomas returned home for a five-month period, which proved to be a very busy time. First the Peace Palace Gardens had been satisfactorily completed by his son and staff but necessitated several visits to The Hague by Thomas for the final stages.

For Mrs. Aitken of Bodelywddan Castle, North Wales, Mawson replanned the upper part of the gardens behind the Castle, and carried out some necessary improvements on a very difficult site. The soil was sparse, resting upon limestone, demanding great care and knowledge in the choice of shrubs and plants; but a fair measure of success was achieved.

Important extensions were planned to the gardens at The Hill, Hampstead, for his client, now Sir William Lever, and also during this time, he planned a superb garden for Mr. Hoyle at Above Beck, Grasmere .

Chapter 13

BRITAIN WITH A HINT OF JAPAN

Grasmere. Stone Arthur is the peak up which William & Dorothy Wordsworth loved to climb. Dorothy named it 'William's Peak'.
Above Beck sits at the foot of Stone Arthur.

After creating a very grand, winged-wall entrance to the sweeping driveway of the house, Above Beck, stands as perfect today as the day it was built almost a hundred years ago. The plan was to give Mr. Hoyle a very gentle access from the house to the elevation of a grand level terrace walk across the bottom of the fell, "Stone Arthur". The repetition of a few steps followed by a length of gently rising pathway, led Mr. Hoyle onto the flat, slate-floored terrace. Below the terrace level was an eight feet high stone retaining wall, still perfect today. At each end of the terrace was a stone-pillared Summer House, providing places of rest and shelter. The interior of each

Left: The graduated steps leading to the slate-floored terrace on the fellside.

The slate-floored terrace, which led to the second summer house.

51

The Life of Thomas Hayton Mawson

The stone retaining wall to the terrace.

Bridge crossing 'above beck'.

summer-house was panelled in oak. The terrace then crosses a small stream over which a balustraded bridge was built ending in a walk-in semi-circular stone buttress on either side. The western buttress provides a viewpoint across to Grasmere and the Easdale Valley and, in those days, from the eastern buttress was a view of the rockery filled with Alpine plants, along the bottom of the fell, to the north. The stream, or in Lakeland terms, the beck, running under the bridge, was captured to form a small lake on the fellside, before continuing on its way. Around this stream and lake area, Mawson planted many different types of maple which reflect on the lake surface, capturing a Japanese Style area of peace and tranquillity, which was to become a very popular trend in the following years. To climb "Stone Arthur" which forms the background to this haven on the hill was a favourite walk of William and Dorothy Wordsworth when they were living in Dove Cottage, 1799-1808, only a few hundred yards south of the site later to be chosen for the erection of Above Beck. They would have passed by the source of Greenhead Ghyll and the unfinished sheepfold, which was so much a feature in Wordsworth's poem "Michael", countless times. So fond of this walk were they that Dorothy named Stone Arthur, William's Peak and William's thoughts of this beloved fell moved him to wax lyrical with a poem dedicated to it, beginning,

> *There is an Eminence,…of these our hills*
> *The last that parleys with the setting sun;*

The balustraded bridge crossing 'above beck'.

The top of the stone buttress becomes a viewing point for a breathtaking view over Grasmere, at 'Above Beck'.

The Life of Thomas Hayton Mawson

The construction of Above Beck's garden was overseen by Thomas's brother, Robert, making sure that the plan drawn by Thomas was strictly adhered to. The Summer House at the northern end of the terrace has now been sensitively enlarged to become a permanent residence. The two original stone pillars at the front of the summerhouse are left exposed, making a permanent reminder of its origin in Mawson's plan. This beautiful home with its fantastic garden and panoramic view of the lake of Grasmere to the south-west, which leads the eye further to the village of Grasmere nestling under Silverhowe to the west, with Wetherlam in the far distance. One's gaze is carried on into the Easedale valley culminating, to the right, with the huge bulk of Helm Crag guarded on its summit by the "Lion and the Lamb". This haven of beauty has the cosy name of *Wren's Nest*. The very caring owners, Mr. and Mrs. Harrison, nurture every found self-seeded Maple sapling with love and care, ensuring that there are always plenty in reserve to maintain the original Maples of the Mawson planting.

The lake on the fellside, below the balustraded bridge.

The construction of the terrace, 'Above Beck' in 1913. First right is Robert Mawson who over-saw that the work was carried out in accordance with his brother Thomas's plans.

54

The fantastic view from Wren's Nest formerly part of Above Beck Grasmere.

Left: The Mawson Maple seedlings on the terrace at Wren's Nest, ready as replacements when needed.

Right: Part of the Mawson Garden in springtime at Wren's Nest, Grasmere.

The Life of Thomas Hayton Mawson

Very shortly after this, Thomas designed another Japanese Garden for Lord Rea of Gatehouse, a huge stone mansion formerly called Esk Villa, in Eskdale.

The site which Mawson chose for the Japanese garden was a boggy area, which would obviously hold water, to the rear of the mansion. It was in a clearing which surrounded the mansion house, in an area known as 'Giggle Alley', and within walking distance from the house. Mawson was entrusted with the design, not only because he was the foremost landscape-architect of his day, but also, in an adopted sense, a 'local' man. Head-gardener at Gatehouse, John Rainbow, and his son Frederick, carried out the work. Lord Rae enthusiastically enhanced the garden by ordering, from Japan, three tall stone lanterns, said to be three hundred years old, a bronze dragon, a tiered pagoda and a resplendent crane to adorn the water features. A small Teahouse was erected and several Japanese-style bridges linked the islands and promontories. The popularity of the Japanese-style garden really 'took off' after the Japan-Britain Exhibition in 1910. For the intrepid explorer setting out to find this 'lost' treasure, an original four feet wide staircase on a path in the forest indicates the entrance, crowned by a 'man-made' cluster of boulders. Still remaining is quite a large amount of the original planting,…rhododendrons, azaleas, bamboos and of course, maples, giving a canopy of brilliant red and orange leaves in the autumn. It is a sound assumption that the Mawson Nursery in Windermere would supply the shrubs and trees as their catologue of the period showed an abundance of all.

Part of the Lost Japanese Garden at Eskdale Cumberland.

So unusual was the garden that a national newspaper, *"The Graphic"* in 1914, contacted a local archaeologist of high standing, Mary Fair, to record her thoughts on this totally 'different' garden which had recently emerged in Cumberland. Mary was the daughter of the local vicar of Eskdale, and a great friend and associate of W. G. Collingwood with whom she had helped to discover, and uncover, the Roman Fort on Hardknott Pass.

Britain with a Hint of Japan

Autumn colour in the 'Lost Japanese Gardens' of Eskdale.

She wrote; "There is, perhaps, no more beautiful spot in all England than the valley of the Esk, which stretches from the sea to beneath the heights of grim Scafell. The Gatehouse estate midway up this valley, possesses beautiful gardens and a glorious view. On an outlying spur of fell, above the grounds a Japanese garden has lately been called into being as by a magician's wand. The site is ideal: a cup on the hill top, which was formerly a peaty swamp dotted with great boulders and slopes of grey granite, has been transformed into a quaint and beautiful garden."

As it was, with Lady Rea in foreground and guests at the bridge.

Mawson was blessed with the gift of always being able to see beyond the reality. Unfortunately, when Lord Rea died, the whole estate was sold at auction in 1949, including the valuable garden artefacts. At this auction, it was confirmed by Frederick Rainbow, the son of head gardener John

57

Rainbow, that the plans were indeed drawn by Thomas Hayton Mawson. The Japanese garden returned to a wilderness but, fortunately, in 1999, a small band of dedicated workers began to restore the garden and the outlines of its past beauty are now emerging again, especially in Spring and Autumn.

At the same time considerable additions were in progress at Roynton Cottage, on the upper slopes of Rivington Pike near Bolton for Lord Leverhulme.

This was the design of a new gatehouse and a 'Romanesque' bridge, the bridge being purely the input of Lever. This bridge crossed a road on the newly designed hillside, and was much used by visitors as a convenient route to the summit of Rivington Pike, the highest peak in this part of Lancashire.

To enhance the landscape of Lever Park even futher and ever conscious of past history, Lever had employed a handful of stonemasons and labourers, c.1912, to work on building a replica of Liverpool Castle which was the first nucleus of Liverpool city. The site he chose was a hillock on the eastern side of the Lower Rivington Reservoir. It was built to view as a ruin and work progressed slowly over a period of twelve to thirteen years, only for work to finish completely after Lord Leverhulme's death. Today, the ruins have aged and in their maturity look very realistic.

Above:
Painting of Liverpool Castle.

Right:
Aerial view of replica ruins of Liverpool Castle on eastern shore of Lower Rivington Reservoir, commissioned by Lord Leverhulme.

Chapter 14

RETURN TO AMERICA AND CANADA

After months of hard work, without a holiday, even for a day, Thomas sailed again for America for the fourth time, accompanied, this time, by his wife.

The day before he sailed, however, a great shock was in store in the shape of a letter of dismissal from Lord Leverhulme, his best client. It was a stunning blow for Mawson; he felt that the bottom had fallen out of his practice! The letter had been polite in terms of personal regard and goodwill, but Lever regretted the fact that he felt that his interests were not being given the personal attention to which he had become accustomed, due to Mawson's long absences abroad. Mawson could understand the reasonable grounds for annoyance in a client who had always adopted a generous attitude towards him and who annually paid him more for his services than he could ever hope to earn by lecturing or working in America. He recognised Lever's reasonable disappointment in having his important work left in the hands of junior partners, but Thomas also thought that Lever was rating his professional services too high, whilst under-estimating the value of the services which his partners and chief of staff were rendering to him. His first and chief work once on board ship was to draft and redraft a letter of reply. Thomas desperately wanted to maintain, if possible, the mutual regard which had grown up between the two men which rested on several interests which they held in common. He decided to be perfectly frank, and listed the reasons for his latest American trip, which were;

(1) To give his sons wider opportunities and greater responsibilities by removing for a time his personal influence.

(2) That only in this way could his sons come into personal relationship with their clients thus assuring continuity for the practice which it had been Thomas's life's work to promote.

(3) That he was very anxious that the English School of Town Planning should exercise a wide influence in Canada and the colonies, and that for some unaccountable reason T. M. seemed to be one of the chosen apostles whose appeal was exercising an influence.

This letter carried more weight than Thomas had dared hope for, for within two weeks he received a reply which, though it did not cancel his dismissal, asked Thomas to let him know when he was returning and wished him a successful tour.

Thomas again lectured in New York, where he gave three lectures at the Columbia University on "Historic Garden Design". Then on to Toronto, where he gave a week's lectures at the University where the audiences numbered hundreds culminating in a full attendance of about twelve hundred on the last night, when his subject was "Garden Cities and Model Housing for the Working Classes".

The course of lectures served a timely purpose, and the publicity given to them did much to stimulate the adoption of city planning legislation in the Dominion, and the establishment of a lectureship on city planning at the University.

On the evening of his last day of his course of lectures, Mawson received a message from the Premier, Sir R. W. Borden, asking him if he would visit Ottawa again, to discuss prospective work for the Government. This was in regard to the replanning of Banff.

From Ottawa, the next stop was Montreal to lecture in a recently opened Art Gallery to an audience which included some leading architects of the city and a goodly number of professors from McGill University.

Onwards to Halifax, Nova Scotia, where his lecture was "The Principles of City Planning". Whilst there, an architect of some note invited Thomas to plan the campus of the Dalhousie University, recognition indeed! The day following his lecture Thomas spent with the Principal of the University inspecting the site of the new campus, some forty-five acres in all. Before leaving he had made all his rough notes and sketches and collected the necessary data for his lay-out scheme. This was helpful in preparing him for the larger university work to follow.

Returning to Montreal, he had meetings with the architects for the New Houses of Parliament at Regina, Thomas having been commissioned to lay out the surrounding public garden.

The Mawsons proceeded to Winnipeg where Thomas lectured to the Ladies Canadian Club. The next stop was Regina, where Thomas lectured to a very large audience on the principles of city planning. The lecture must have made an impression as, before he left, he was commissioned by the Government to lay out the gardens and park surrounding the Parliament Buildings and also plan a building estate of about three hundred acres.

From Regina they travelled to Saskatoon, where Mawson's business was at the University of Saskatchewan. In collaboration with the architects he had to lay out the entire campus. The campus occupied a well-chosen site on an elevated plateau some three hundred and sixty acres in extent, bounded on the south by the Bow River. The University Governors were ambitious, and decided to plan in advance for the most complete campus in Canada to accommodate 9000 students. Thomas thought it a mistake that the University was not erected at Regina to contribute more to the importance of that city.

Next stop was Calgary where Thomas had a series of lectures to deliver as part of a propaganda campaign under the auspices of the Citizens' League.

The publicity given to these meetings was effectively done for the lectures were attended by large enthusiastic audiences. A resolution in favour of a city plan was sent to the City Council, with a result that Thomas left Calgary with a contract in his pocket to prepare a development plan. Out of the many invitations he received to talk on planning, the only one he accepted was at the nice little city of Medicine Hat, which was situated on the main Canadian Pacific Railroad line. Perhaps they liked the name, or perhaps it was the convenience of its situation. This meeting was rather spoilt by a rather boastful American who tried to monopolise the conversation during the preceding lunch. However, Thomas quietly put him in his place. He got to his feet and began, *"Gentlemen, I must apologise for being a mere Englishman, for according to some of our critics we are rapidly approaching the period of our decline; but so ingrained are our historic associations and our love of industry that from mere force of habit we keep on* doing *things!"*

From Medicine Hat, the next location was Banff, the St. Moritz of the Rockies, to make a first investigatory study of the town site and a wide section of the National Park, which Thomas was to develop, which included the three hot springs and the vermillion lakes. Thomas reminisced, later, *"We stay-at-home islanders have no idea of the glory of our Colonial possessions....in spring and early summer the region is a floral paradise, as are the Alps, with a distinct botanical classification of its own."*

At Banff, the Canadian Pacific, with their usual enterprise, had erected a million-dollar hotel to accommodate the increasing crowds of visitors and, since it was built they had already more than doubled the accommodation.

Having allotted five days of his tour for making his survey, Mawson spent every hour of daylight collecting data, making diagrams and sketches for his plan and report, motoring, and examining the whole site and its immediate environs.

On a tour which must have required a great deal of stamina, they finally took a train for Vancouver, passing through the awe-inspiring Canadian Rockies. Thomas intended to catch up on his writing on the journey but, passing through such amazing country he found it impossible to take his eyes away from the majestic scenery, and work seemed puny and useless in contrast. Thomas afterwards wrote; *"In the presence of these majestic mountains, these sentinels of eternity, the ever-changing wonder of glaciers, white cloud-splitting peaks, roaring torrents, mighty pine forests interspersed with expansive lakes, one is struck dumb with awe and reverence. Oh for a modicum of John Ruskin's powers of description!"*

This trip extended to just over three months and constituted great educational value and, furthermore, the value of the confidence placed in him and the unbounded kindness of the Canadian people overwhelmed him.

Thomas Mawson may be placed in this first generation of British Town

Planners who were to have a significant impact on the development of early town planning practices in Canada. His book, "Civic Art", published in 1911, was widely read and helped to establish his reputation as an authority on civic design. Mawson's success as a landscape designer enlarged his horizons and he added to his credentials those of town planner and architect.

On returning to England, Thomas found that Lord Lever, who had earlier dismissed him, wished to meet him. With a little apprehension, Thomas called at the time and place appointed. He need not have worried, for he was met in a most friendly way and asked to carry on as before, as Lever had realised that in his sons Thomas was fortunate to have partners who would loyally uphold the standard of work set by their father. Thus was achieved one of the objects, which justified his long absences from home in working on commissions in other countries.

Very soon, Thomas found himself planning extensive garden improvements for John R. Barlow, Esq., of Greenthorn, Edgeworth, near Bolton, who was head of one of the most important cotton-manufacturing concerns in Lancashire and a partner of Mr. William Hoyle for whom he had already worked at Above Beck, Grasmere. A most successful part of Greenthorn garden was the conversion of a formal stream, hemmed in between irregularly built walls, into a series of rocky cascades. A stone-built bridge was also constructed. At one time, Thomas was engaged by four gentlemen concerned in cotton, at the same time.

An important matter which needed Thomas's immediate attention was to complete arrangements for a course of lectures to be delivered at the Melbourne, Brisbane, Perth, Sydney, and Adelaide Universities, in Australia. He was to give a course of six lectures at each University, for which he would be paid six hundred pounds, inclusive of expenses; not a very large fee, but a splendid introduction to the Government, which desired to consult Mawson about town-planning. Meanwhile, the staff at home assured Thomas that the preliminary schemes for Regina, Calgary, Banff and Vancouver would be all ready to submit, as arranged, in the autumn.

Chapter 15

A FORTUITOUS MEETING, AND THE ANTIPODES POSTPONED

Whilst in London, for a weekend, in 1913, Mawson met Sir Hubert Herkomer, R.A., who asked Thomas if he would come to his home, Lululaund in Bushy, which Thomas found was a Bohemian Castle, and advise him on his garden. They walked the garden together, discussing many points and when they came to talk of the probable costs, Sir Hubert readily agreed. Finally, he remarked: *"We still have to settle your fees and I am going to make a suggestion which I hope you will accept. I think,"* he said, *"you ought to have your portrait painted; my price for this would be six hundred guineas. Let's swop. I'll do your portrait whilst you design my rose garden and we'll call it quits."* Thomas readily agreed, confident he had made a bargain! From this bargain emerged the portrait, the most famous likeness of Thomas Hayton Mawson, and always chosen to represent him, as on the front cover of this book.

The last portrait painted by Herkomer was that of Governor Brown of Regina, to whom Thomas had shown a photograph of *his* portrait. Governor Brown wired Herkomer to ask if he could paint his portrait and got in reply the following message: "If you can come immediately, I think I can do it." Mr. Brown started for England the next day, and was just in time, for his last sitting concluded Herkomer's life work. The distinguished artist died a few days later. As Mr. Brown remarked, it almost seemed as if he had had a premonition when he sent his cable. Thomas felt Herkomer's loss keenly. During their short aquaintance, they were drawn closely together. Thomas felt *that he was one of the most versatile men he had ever met; his buoyancy was contagious and he was a most delightful, companionable man, and a true artist....a Bohemian by natural birth and a Bohemian by temperament.*

As already planned, Thomas proposed to travel to Australia *via* Vancouver where he planned to spend two months discussing his preliminary plans with several Governmental and municipal clients. Mawson's two sons, Edward Prentice and Cliffe, with the staff, had done much of the preparation of the Canadian town plans, often interpreting their father's proposals from the roughest of sketches and, with perfect success, showing how well they were trained.

When Thomas arrived at St. John, New Brunswick, he found a cable from his son waiting for him, stating that His Majesty King Constantine of Greece wished to consult him about the royal gardens in Athens and a park system for his capital. This was great news and called for immediate action. The possibility of working in this world-famous city under royal patronage was irresistible. Hoping and believing that his Australian clients would see in this call one of the greatest compliments which could be paid to British Art, Thomas cabled to them for permission to postpone his trip. At the same time he cabled to his son asking him to proceed to Greece at once with whatever assistants he required for the preparation of surveys and the collection of data. In the mean time, Thomas would get through his work in Canada as quickly as possible and join him in Athens on completion. Mawson's duties in Canada took about six weeks and, with extensive notes on town sites to be re-planned, he was able to take them direct to his office in Vancouver, which had already been established under the direction of second son, John William, with nephew Robert Mattocks as chief of staff.

Returning home at the end of May, Thomas found that Edward Prentice had just about completed the designs for the royal gardens in Athens and had obtained approval for his preliminary basic plans before leaving the city. The King and Queen had been most interested in the work and had given interviews almost daily, giving helpful discussion on every feature as the plan progressed.

Their Majesties had taken Edward Prentice to their villa at Tatoi and discussed the need for a new villa, larger and better, to be built on a plateau somewhat elevated above the existing one. They also instructed him to prepare plans for their burial ground, which occupied the site of a beautiful knoll not far from Tatoi, though secluded from the villa. From this knoll the view to the southwest was of Athens and the Acropolis in the distance. King Constantine wished to enclose this ground suitably and lay it out in the form of a simple terrace connected by a wide central path leading to the small Byzantine chapel which was perched on the highest part.

At the end of June, their royal patron and family came to Eastbourne on their annual holiday in England, where they always stayed at the Grand Hotel. A date was arranged for Mawson and his son to meet them there. Firstly, Edward introduced his father to the Court Chamberlain, Count Mercati, whom Thomas found very friendly and helpful from then on. In the afternoon, Count Mercati introduced Thomas to King Constantine and Queen Sophia of Greece.

The King was a keen gardener, whilst the Queen said she was longing to see Thomas at work on re-housing the working classes in Athens, where the conditions were deplorable.

King Constantine finally approved the plans for the royal gardens and it was arranged that Thomas would meet him in Athens in September, calling at Corfu 'en-route' with a view to improving the gardens around the royal palace there and to offer any suggestions for the improvement of the town of Corfu. Futhermore, the king said he would hope to commission Thomas for improvement plans of Athens itself.

In the interval between June and September, Thomas returned to his first love of private gardens in Britain, visiting clients, which he found a delightful and restful change after the heavier toils of public work. *"There was apparently*

A Fortuitous Meeting and the Antipodes Postponed

no end to garden making, Mawson stated, *for when one part is improved it shows up disparagingly the other parts. If the owners of gardens only knew at the outset how far their initial experiments would lead them, their courage might surely fail".*

King Constantine I of Greece ruled from 1913 until he was forced to abdicate in 1917 due to virtual civil war.
He was restored again as king in 1920, only to abdicate again in 1922.

Above:
King Constantine I of Greece
1913-1917 1920-22.

Right:
Queen Sophia of Greece, formerly Princess of Prussia.

Chapter 16

COMINGS AND GOINGS
1913-1914

Thomas and Edward Prentice left for Athens at the end of August, 1913, travelling *via* Paris, Rome, Brindisi and Corfu, 'the jewel of the Adriatic', and were over-awed by the beauty and depth of colour of this island which they had thought must be exaggerated in posters, yet, "Every element of the picturesque was here embodied", Thomas wrote. Nevertheless, six major improvements were planned for the town and as Edward had called here previously on his return from Athens for the purpose of collecting data for the planning preparation, with which Thomas fully agreed, they were able to present a scheme for Corfu to the king immediately on their arrival in Athens. Any amendments needed were done through discussion, reaching satisfaction on both sides.

After this work was completed the king then talked of the things he wished to see in their plans for Athens. Among them was a new parliament building; a new dignified union railway station of ample proportions and the removal of all the shacks and hovels which had grown around the base of the Acropolis. The king stressed that it was very important to impress tourists with their care. Last named was his pet hobby, of a wide belt of land for afforestation round the capital, offering shade.

They toured around the capital together discussing plans. In a pause for the view, Thomas, noticing the orange trees ladened with fruit, remarked light-heartedly that the boys of Athens must be peculiarly honest and told the king that, in England even fences round the fruit trees did not keep the boys out. "Boys", replied the king, *"are the same the world over,...these are bitter oranges!"* The tour finished, and the king drove back to the palace at a lightning speed, making the two Englishmen relieved to alight. Everyone seemed to know that the king was at the wheel and scurried out of the way.

Planting the trees commenced promptly the next day. Several wagon-loads of pines, cypresses and shrubs had been deposited, and a squad of men with picks and spades had been requisitioned to dig the holes and plant the trees as they set them out. A crowd soon collected to see their King and Queen setting out trees and shrubs so enthusiastically! Thomas Mawson and son left Athens with a contract for all the work to be done, duly signed and delivered.

For the two weeks following their return home, Thomas again visited English and Scottish clients. By the third week in November he was again on his way to Canada, *via* New York, to present their revised plan for Banff to the Parks Department of the Dominion Government and to submit their designs for Coal Harbour and Stanley Park to the Parks Commission of Vancouver, B.C.

Comings and Goings

After Vancouver, Thomas arranged a visit to Victoria, B.C., to inspect and plan new town sites for the B.C. Electric Company, the James Estate on the east coast of the island and the Meadlands Estate on the west coast. During his stay he had many opportunities for meeting the Premier, Sir Richard McBride. Before leaving Victoria, Thomas was asked to address the City Council and the public on the need and advantages of city planning for Victoria.

On his return to Vancouver, Thomas was engaged with Professor Laird of Philadelphia and Professor Darley of McGill University, Montreal, upon the preparation of a comprehensive report and plan for the new British Columbia University at Point Grey.

The site, consisting of three hundred acres, was selected by the recommendation of the aforesaid trio, as it occupied a magnificent position on the western extremity of Point Grey and would be in full view of all the shipping passing north or south or entering Vancouver. The university buildings were designed to be worthy and impress beholders and, at night, in the centre would be a tower brilliantly lighted and rising to a height of three hundred feet. It was planned to be a dominating feature and a landmark from all directions.

This completed Mawson's studies for the fourth university campus upon which he had worked in Canada.

Arriving home in the middle of January, 1914, Thomas immediately set to work upon town-planning projects, for which his son E. Prentice Mawson had done much preparatory work. Of course, a lot of the attention focused on Athens, as Thomas knew this commission was probably the pinnacle of his ambitions and would give a great boost to his reputation, worldwide.

In the home department Thomas was now engaged in several planting schemes, valuing the help from his third son, James Radcliffe, known to all as 'Cliffe', who had developed a keen sense of the possibilities of the horticultural side of their work. He had a natural aptitude for the subject and a keen love of nature. 'Cliffe' had been schooled in art at the Ecole des Beaux Arts in Paris and had a genial manner and a happy disposition. His father had high hopes for Cliffe's prospects. There would have been many proud fathers in the land at the beginning of 1914 with similar hopes for their sons' prospects, many happy parents who had no idea of the horrors to come.

The 16th of March found Thomas lecturing before the Civic League of Antwerp on "The Principles of Landscape Architecture Applied to the Development of the City Plan". Evidently the Civic League wished to learn about English methods with a view to making their own new parks and boulevards as attractive as possible. In the evening, he lectured to about four hundred people in English. They seemed to understand and, when slides were shown from time to time, they applauded enthusiastically.

From Antwerp, Thomas proceeded to Paris *en-route* to Athens, calling at Corfu on the way. Arrangements were made by Mr. Samuel Waring, an old friend and client of Mawson, for meeting him in Paris, so that he may travel on to Athens with Thomas and, when they called at Corfu, Mr. Waring would introduce Mawson to the Kaiser at his villa.

On arrival at Brindisi, keen disappointment awaited the couple. They were informed that the Kaiser had received an urgent call to Berlin and that he had left Corfu the previous day. The news filled them with dark forebodings, for they felt unease at the Kaiser's sudden departure. They were half inclined to return home there and then but, after a night's sleep, decided to go on to Corfu. The following day, Mr. Waring, still apprehensive of trouble, decided to return home that same evening.

Thomas journeyed on and took a boat to Patras thence on to Athens where his stay extended to about five weeks, during which time he had constant meetings with the King and Queen. During one of these meetings, Thomas was accompanied by his eldest son who had been in Athens for some time and, now, most of the interviews with the Queen were about the re-housing of the working classes under conditions of comfort and decency.

It was arranged that, on Thomas's return to England, he should immediately prepare a number of housing proposals for submission and approval pending their Majesties' arrival in Eastbourne in June. Before returning home, Thomas and Edward made an exhaustive study of the railway and tram systems towards which, at this time, the Government were prepared to make substantial subsidies.

As a last gesture prior to leaving Athens, Thomas gave a lecture which was attended by the King, members of the Royal Family and many of the Ministers and Heads of Government departments. His principal object was to endeavour to incite the authorities to secure an ample water supply, without which it was little use considering park systems or indeed any housing extensions. In fact, Thomas ventured to point out, the whole town-planning scheme for the city should be based upon provision of utilities for cleanliness and decency and that they had been discussing this for forty years, spending large sums of money on experts but they were no further forward than they had been at the beginning.

Chapter 17

THE WAR YEARS

Father and son returned home to work with their office staff in Lancaster, which had now grown to thirty assistants, mostly young fellows loyal to their chief and keen in their ideals. The auditor assured them in his annual visit, that the firm was financially sound.

Thomas Hayton Mawson and some of the Lancaster 'High Street House' staff, in 1913, named as far as is known by Thomas Prentice Mawson. 2nd left, Edward Prentice Mawson. 3rd left, James Radcliffe Mawson. 4th left, Thomas Hayton Mawson. Small girl's face left ctr, Hannah Richardson. Young boy next to her, T. Wearing Pennington. Top back right with beard, John Dyer. Two below him with bow tie, Bill Dean. 2nd down from top right, John Shaw. On his left, James Crossland. 1st right, thought to be Howard Grubb. Hannah Richardson worked for three generations of Mawsons.

At the end of July 1914, however, doubts for the future were ever increasing. Some said that war, if it came, would clear the air. Others said that war, if it came, would be over in three months and end war for all time. July ended with depressing days.

69

On the morning of 4th August, 1914, came the announcement that England was at war with Germany. Thomas wrote;

"As I went to the office, the world seemed suddenly to have come to a standstill, with an entire absence of that purposeful business hurry to which we are daily accustomed. In its place there was an awed hush amongst the groups of whispering townsmen along the kerbstone, whilst knots of women stood at their doors talking in unusually quiet tones. Then would pass along companies of young fellows on their way to enlist. Their buoyancy was in strange contrast to the demeanour of their elders.

Arriving at the office, I found that every unmarried man, including my third son, James Radcliffe, had marched off to the Town Hall to enlist—a record in patriotism which I imagine few offices in the country could surpass. In one sense I was proud of the fact, yet in another way it was heart-breaking to see the growth of years and organisation breaking up, with no certainty of its ever being got together again. Two of my young men were Quakers, but they joined up, and later one of them won the Croix-de-Guerre, and the other gave his life".

Fortunately for this father and the practice, his eldest son and partner, Edward Prentice Mawson, was rejected on medical grounds. The second son, John, who was in charge of the Canadian office, joined up as soon as the local forces could arrange for his training.

After the declaration of war, it was only a natural sequence of events that clients from every quarter wrote stopping all work or curtailing it to a minimum. The dim outlook was that there was scarcely sufficient work in the office for the remaining members of staff. The men who were left were the older men, knowledgeable and indispensable for re-construction when times allowed. Knowing that Thomas Mawson would not dispense with their services unless circumstances forced the issue, the remaining members of staff, of their own free will, proposed that they should take a cut in their salaries by as much as one third. This arrangement proved unsound, for the staff found that with soaring costs of living, they needed more, not less, in their pay- packets. However, their expression of goodwill was very much appreciated by their employer who, in return, made great efforts to keep them employed.

There was still the completion of plans for Athens, Regina and Banff to work upon, whilst some of Mawson's most faithful clients with patriotic sentiments, decided to go ahead with certain works, thus supplying the much needed employment. Foremost among these was Thomas's faithful friend, Lord Leverhulme.

In these days of reduced activity, Thomas concentrated on collecting material for two books he had long been planning and Athens provided material for a third. The publishers used by Mawson, *Batsford*, stated quite definitely that no works of this nature could be launched until after the war,

The War Years

as the cost of printing would be absolutely prohibitive. Thomas continued with the work thinking that if he never finished them himself, he hoped his successors would.

As the war with all its horrors continued, more and more men were needed and encouraged to fight for their country. This call further reduced the staff of the Lancaster office, as some of the much younger men became eligible to defend their country. The London and Vancouver offices, having lost their staff, became mere postal addresses. This resulted in all the Mawson firm's work being concentrated in the Lancaster office only. From a staff of thirty personnel, the office now housed eleven namely Thomas himself, Edward Prentice, his son, two pupils, four men over military age, a lady secretary, a typist and a book-keeper.

Wishing to help the war effort in any way possible, Thomas thought of offering his services to the Ministry of Munitions who were at this time laying out a number of munition villages, such as that at Gretna Green. He obtained an introduction to the secretary of the Department of Construction, who received him as if he were looking for a contractor's job.

Mawson gave details of his organisation and told the secretary that they were ready and anxious for work and that he and his son would give their services free, adding that the Ministry could take over the staff and offices on its own terms. Thomas left his name and address. After waiting a month he contacted the secretary again, having heard that other schemes were going ahead, but was told that the work was 'already in hand.'

One evening, at his club, Mawson met a young man who had made a lot of money out of the Ministry of Munitions, and who was later knighted for 'his sacrifices'. "Mawson," he said, "I heard of that offer of yours; but why did you make it? You surely knew it would be rejected! They knew that you had an organisation which would be useful to them, but you made it impossible by offering your services gratis. If you had boldly said, 'Gentlemen, I am at your service, and my terms are two thousand pounds per year', they would have accepted you on the spot." His obvious look of success seemed to give truth to the statement.

Early in the year of 1915, James Radcliffe Mawson, always known as 'Cliffe', third son of Thomas Hayton Mawson, had joined the Pals Brigade of the 5th Kings Own Royal Lancaster Regiment. *Pals Brigade* was a term used for young men from the same village or town who joined the Military at the same time, and the Military endeavoured to let them serve together, whenever possible. Cliffe had completed his training and was detailed for Foreign Service. His father wrote, *"He came home for a few days, bright, optimistic and eager, assured we had got the Germans on the run and that he would be back home again by the end of June. He left us amid cheers and tears. Then came home breezy letters, but each succeeding letter a little more wistful than the last. In another letter he had said: 'The morning is fine and the country is beautiful; every-*

where the hedgerows are draped in tenderest green. The birds are singing their sweetest, oblivious to the horrors of this terrible war.' In what was to prove his last letter he told us: 'The men are splendid, and beyond all praise. Whatever you can do for our wounded, I am sure you will do…nothing is too good for these brave fellows.'" These extracts were written by his father on account of their sequel.

"His end came soon after. He fell near Poperinghe on April 23rd, 1915. So ended one of my fondest hopes, for he had a wonderful grasp of the possibilities of his profession. He also possessed irresistible charm of manner, and was at the same time a diplomat who generally got his way."

"And he was a humorist; 'What do you think of Herkomer's portrait of your father?' asked a lady visitor.

'It is just splendid, and so life-like that I often talk to it.'

'Talk to it, Cliffe? Whatever do you say?'

And, clasping his hands in an attitude of appeal, he replied: 'I say, Please father, give me a rise.' And next week and onwards his allowance envelope contained an extra five shillings."

"I might tell many more such stories, but must keep them locked up as sacred memories."

Cliffe is buried in Perth Cemetery, sometimes known as the 'China Wall Cemetery', located almost two miles east of Ypres town centre and half a mile from a crossroads that the troops knew as 'Hell-Fire Corner'. The reason for the name of 'Perth' is unknown, but 'China Wall' is from the communication trench, which ran through that area, which the soldiers jokingly called 'The Great Wall of China'. After the Armistice, graves were brought in from the battlefields around Ypres and 'China Wall Cemetery' now contains 2,791 Commonwealth servicemen of the First World War.

The Cemetery was designed by Edward Lutyens.

From Cliffe's letters, already quoted, his father began a mission for action for the wounded and disabled who were already returning in vast numbers, a large proportion of whom were rendered unfit to follow their former occupations.

Plans that were already half-way through for a Memorial Park in Shadwell were quickly completed and presented to London County Council as a gift, to get on with more pressing work. Surprisingly, the gift was returned with a letter curtly informing Mawson that they "had their own landscape gardeners." To this Mawson replied that what *he* was offering was the work of a landscape-architect and not that of a landscape gardener. *"The poor man did not know the difference"*, wrote Mawson.

Getting nowhere with appeals for money in England, Mawson decided to pursue contacts he had made in America and Canada, so he and his wife

The War Years

once more set sail on what was to be their last trip to America. At that time, early October 1915, America was still neutral. The voyage was a long one, the weather stormy, and sailing by St. Paul to minimise the submarine risks was long and tedious.

During a long lecture tour, including New York, one weekend was spent at Bryn Mawr, a splendidly designed ladies college occupying an enviously elevated site. It was here, at Bryn Mawr, that Woodrow Wilson, then the present President of the United States of America, started his previous career as a teacher, conducting classes in literature and history for six years. In those pre-President days there was no indication of his future fame or his love that was to develop for the English Lake District and his great friendship with the Lake District Artist, Fred Yates, of Rydal. It was in Fred Yates's humble stone cottage at Rydal that Woodrow Wilson spent many extremely happy vacations with Fred, his wife Emily and daughter Mary. When Woodrow Wilson was inaugurated as the 28th President of the United States on 4th March, 1913, he invited Fred Yates, from the tiny hamlet of Rydal, to the White House as a guest. As a sign of President Wilson's sincere friendship, he donated his Inaugural Flag to Fred Yates to bring home to the English Lake District. For the remainder of the Yate's lives they draped this American flag from their highest point (which was the bedroom window) on every 4th of July, American Independence Day. This story would surely have been recalled by Thomas Mawson during his stay at Bryn Mawr.

Woodrow Wilson's inaugural flag draped across the Yates's cottage at Rydal.

Thomas and Anna Mawson returned to England on the English ship, 'Orduna', sailing from New York on the 16th December 1915. Great was their relief to dock safely in Liverpool on 26th December 1915.

Chapter 18

'COMETH THE OCCASION, COMETH THE MAN'

Thomas continued to campaign for settlements for the shattered men returning to the nation in the aftermath of war. He made strong pleas for the provision of old-fashioned handicrafts and trades, and had the idea that, in the first instance, one or two older villages could be devoted to the growing of young trees to replenish the areas deforested by the war. Other villages could be growing flowers or creating bulb farms. Also basket-making or other such open-air occupations could be provided for tubercular or shell-shocked men. Toy making, pencil manufacture, printing books for children and doll making were all suggested.

The word 'segregation' had been used very frequently and Mawson came across it time and time again.

The idea of segregating the shattered men and their families from the rest of the community was not liked in many places and the word 'segregation' became a political issue.

In vain Mawson pointed out that in all of our lives we came across the principle of segregation, in politics, in worship, in jobs and in schools. As he travelled on the train he knew that the men who lived in Crewe had a population segregated for the production and repair of railway stock, and when travelling through Rugby, boys were segregated to attend that famous school. Finally, when he arrived in London, if he wished to consult a doctor, he found the segregation of medical men installed in Harley Street and Wimpole Street, and so-on, and so-on.

Thomas found that fighting Government objections was like waging war with the hydra-headed monster of mythology,….for every head you chop off, another three come in its place. Opposition only increased his determination. Thomas decided to write a book describing his proposals in more detail, with fully illustrated plans and perspective drawings. The cost, quite apart from the printing and binding, and the time taken to prepare it for the press, was considerable.

The book was titled, "An Imperial Obligation" with 'Industrial Villages for partially Disabled Service Men' as a sub-title. A first edition of six hundred copies was published and circulated privately in February 1917. They were sent to members of the Royal Family, Ministers and important members of both Houses of Parliament. Other people who were to receive a copy were church dignitaries, poets, writers, artists, mayors of boroughs, leaders of industry and commerce, also Colonial Premiers and foreign Ambassadors in London, with a request for criticism and suggestions.

The response was amazing! Almost every Minister sent his

congratulations, as also did bishops, other church leaders, university professors and writers.

The only criticisms offered were a few on 'segregation', the dying echoes of the Ministry of Pensions!

A short selection of some correspondence to Mawson of the time can be quoted, as follows;

"Lord Lansdown wrote :

We ought all of us to be grateful to those who make, as you have made, a determined effort to grapple with the difficulties of the problems which will have to be solved in dealing with our disabled soldiers…..I do not think we should get on at all unless we had dreamers amongst us, and your 'dream' seems to me a very bright and attractive one.

General Sir William Robertson :

I can assure you that any practical solution for meeting the necessities and deserts of the men who have fought in the war has my utmost sympathy and best wishes for success.

John Oxenham :

I agree absolutely….If your fine scheme can be carried out, it may save Britain from some of the evil times which I fear await her when the settlement comes, which may be more of an unsettlement than anything we have yet seen in this country…Every good wish to your great work. Carry it through somehow and you will deserve well of the world.

But the best letter of all came from Herbert Storey, D.C.L.

Your scheme attracts me so much that, with the approval of other members of my family, I propose to make possible a practical beginning by offering as a gift the residence of my father, the late Sir Thomas Storey, along with fifteen acres of excellent building land on which to erect cottages and workshops. The only condition I make is that preference should be given to Lancaster men and any disabled member of the 5th King's Own Regiment."

Mawson calculated that this splendid gift was to the value of at least £15,000, which would be nearly three quarters of a million pounds today.

Scores of other letters urged him to go ahead. He had a new, revised edition of the book printed compiled from the criticism and appreciation. Then six precious months were lost in the hope that Lloyd George would consent to write a foreword for the book.

Men sympathetic to the cause who were in almost daily contact with Lloyd George used all their persuasive power to obtain this invaluable service but this, also failed. The reason was never known. At this point, someone inquired if they had asked Field Marshal Sir Douglas Haig. The idea was immediately acted upon. Mawson received the following sympathetic response, from General Headquarters, France:

"*Dear Mr. Mawson,*

While I greatly appreciate your kindness in sending me advanced proofs of your book, "An Imperial Obligation", I regret that, so far, my many engagements have prevented my giving them the attention I hope to at no very distant date, for I feel that the subject which you have tackled, the amelioration of the lot of those our countrymen on whom this war has placed the dreadful burden of life-long disablement, is not only the most worthy to which it is possible to bend one's energies, but one which should receive immediate attention if we are to be ready for the emergency before it becomes overwhelming.

This much, however, I can say as a 'Foreword' to your book: Any scheme honestly conceived and energetically and skilfully pursued for such a cause, is one which I feel confident will command the practical sympathy of our countrymen, and, as such, will have my hearty approval.

21st June 1917. Yours faithfully, D. Haig, FM."

The second edition of "An Imperial Obligation" was a much more attractive book than the first and Thomas acknowledged the help of his secretary and of his son as illustrator for their contribution in this. While awaiting publication, Mawson spent a great deal of his time getting together an organisation with an executive committee, which finally consisted of Warwick H. Draper, Thomas H. Mawson, Walter S. Rowntree, Gordon Selfridge, Herbert L. Storey, Samuel Waring and William H. Whiting.

When the book finally appeared it received splendid notices and reviews, and many influential people were becoming interested in that which Mawson was striving to achieve. The Ministry of Pensions, however, continued to remain hostile to the scheme outlined in "An Imperial Obligation" and some potential 'backers' dropped out, as they were unwilling to act in opposition to the Ministry of Pensions.

The press gave its approval.

"Mr. Mawson's scheme…….is both ideal and practical." **The Times.**

"Here is the book of a dream made practical." **The Morning Post.**

"Here is no mere visionary: his eye knoweth what his hand can achieve." **The Daily Chronicle.**

Mawson wrote, "*As a town-planner having to deal with sociological and collective schemes of habitation every day and having made a wide study of village life, both industrially and in the matter of habitations and gardens, I could give the assurance that, once the initial support was forthcoming, the professional guidance and the handicrafts would not be far behind. Being an old member of the Art Workers Guild, I knew that its members (who represent the best-informed minds of all the principal arts and crafts in the country) could be relied upon for advice, help and support."*

At this time the domestic policy of the country was concentrated on housing.

"Why not therefore", Thomas argued, *"begin by housing the wounded men and their families in these villages, say twenty to fifty families in each, and providing for their training and employment in those crafts dependent upon the building trade? Thus one village colony could be devoted to the making of lead lights and ornamental glazing; another colony to the making of fibrous plaster for plain and decorative work; another to fitments for plumbers, and so on, the whole grouped together for publicity, collection of orders, and the distribution of the finished products through some central place in the adjoining town.*

This is regional planning for the purpose of production and distribution. This plan would have involved very limited segregation".

Thomas's chief object was to induce the Ministry of Pensions to see the possibilities of constructive effort on behalf of the wounded servicemen. This unfortunately failed.

Meanwhile, Government Departments in allied countries sent for further copies of the book and advice on the best manner of carrying out the recommendations contained therein. A good result from Thomas's book was that property owners began to offer sites for villages, occasionally with a view to donating, but more often with a desire to sell one. All were investigated and reported upon by Mawson and Mr. Storey. They also decided to promote interest in their proposals in important country centres by Thomas giving lectures, illustrated by many interesting slides.

The committee decided to go ahead on still bolder lines, to study six projects, including the one of Lancaster, dealing with proposed developments in various parts of the country.

Mawson, accompanied by Mr. James Crossland, his ever faithful secretary and photographer, who was as enthusiastic as himself in the project, travelled long distances visiting sites, making surveys, taking photographs and stating the possible use for each. Next to the importance to housing, attention was given to afforestation. Promises to re-afforest our denuded countrysides were always applauded,

Meathop, near Grange-over-Sands Mawson considered an excellent site for this purpose. Why not establish forest/tree nurseries for shell-shocked men and those in the early stages of tuberculosis, to supply the Government's promised afforestation policy? Meathop Flats presented

an ideal opportunity, with its five hundred acres of flat rich land, with easily worked sandy soil. This was becoming derelict owing to the protecting seawall having been broken through by an abnormally high tide and left un-repaired. This property, including extensive farm buildings, was offered for £2,500 (£116,000 today) and formed an ideal site for an afforestation nursery and bulb farm, the soil and climate being in every way equal to that of the bulb-growing district in Holland.

Mr. Crossland produced an illustrated pamphlet under the title of "Afforestation and the disabled." This pamphlet made an immediate appeal to the press and Lord Leverhulme, Mawson's old friend and client, immediately sent a cheque for £250 (£11,600 today) Foresters gave very good reports for approving the scheme, suggesting that half the land should be devoted to bulb growing. Figures, when worked out, showed that they could have a splendid nursery ready for immediate cultivation at twenty-five pounds per acre, including extensive buildings and farm houses and cottages for the use of the estate manager, packing, etc., etc.

The Board of Agriculture sent up a recommendation to the treasury to grant the money but, by a stroke of bad luck, the application was presented on the day upon which Lloyd George introduced his economy campaign, and was promptly turned down.

Mawson had no hesitation in saying that if the Government had risked the comparatively small outlay, and if they had got a good subsidy in aid of the homesteads, Lancashire and Yorkshire would, in their patriotic generosity, have met the bill, and this beneficent enterprise might now be a thriving business and a great benefit to the country.

Chapter 19

THE 'STOREY' OF THE WESTFIELD MILITARY VILLAGE, LANCASTER

The idea which led to the founding of Westfield War Memorial Village in Lancaster was undoubtedly originated by Thomas Hayton Mawson, whose efforts could never have succeeded without the generosity of Mr. Herbert Lushington Storey.

He built no cenotaph; instead, Thomas Hayton Mawson planned a village for the living, in memory of the dead.

The neat little cottages in the centre of Lancaster are a silent tribute to the men who made the supreme sacrifice, (including Mawson's third son, James Radcliffe Mawson), and a tribute to the thoughtfulness of one man and the generosity of another.

The Armistice, which was to come in 1918, was twelve months away when the idea of homes instead of monuments was born. Writing in his book, "An Imperial Obligation", which was published in 1917, Mawson said that the way to remember those who had died for their country and to pay a debt of gratitude to those whose bodies and minds had been broken in conflict, was to build carefully planned village settlements for disabled men and able-bodied men.

The suggestion appealed to Herbert Lushington Storey, DL., of "Bailrigg", Lancaster who, following the example and work of his ancestors, had played a great part in the industrial development of Lancaster. He saw the possibility of such a village settlement taking shape on the fifteen acres of land which surrounded "Westfield", a great stone house which had been the

The centrepiece of Westfield War Memorial Village with red gate of first finished cottage in background.

The Life of Thomas Hayton Mawson

The first cottage completed in Westfield Village. The Herbert Storey Cottage.

Plaque inside porch of the Herbert Storey Cottage.

THIS COTTAGE WAS ERECTED BY
HERBERT LUSHINGTON STOREY ESQ.
D.L., J.P. OF BAILRIGG.
AS A THANK OFFERING FOR THE
SAFE RETURN OF HIS SON
CAPTAIN KENNETH STOREY
WHO SERVED WITH THE 20TH HUSSAR REGT
IN THE GREAT WAR 1914-1918.

Lintel stone above the doorway to the first finished cottage.

THE WAR MEMORIAL VILLAGE
· LANCASTER ·
THIS STONE WAS LAID BY
THE RIGHT HONOURABLE
LORD RICHARD CAVENDISH
C.B. C.M.G.
15TH NOVEMBER 1919.

HERBERT 19 STOREY 19 COTTAGE

The Storey of the 'Westfield Military Village', Lancaster

> THE WESTFIELD WAR MEMORIAL VILLAGE FOUNDED IN GRATEFUL REMEMBRANCE OF THE SACRIFICE MADE BY THE KING'S OWN ROYAL LANCASTER REGIMENT THE LANCASTER BATTERIES OF ARTILLERY AND OTHER LANCASTRIANS IN THE GREAT WAR 1914—1918 THE CHILDREN OF SIR THOMAS STOREY GAVE THE PROPERTY THE COTTAGES WERE BUILT BY PUBLIC AND INDIVIDUAL SUBSCRIPTION THE VILLAGE WAS DESIGNED BY THOMAS HAYTON MAWSON

Above Left: The plaque on the plinth of the war memorial, Westfield Military Village.

Above: The front door to Bailrigg showing initials of H.L. & E.M. Storey

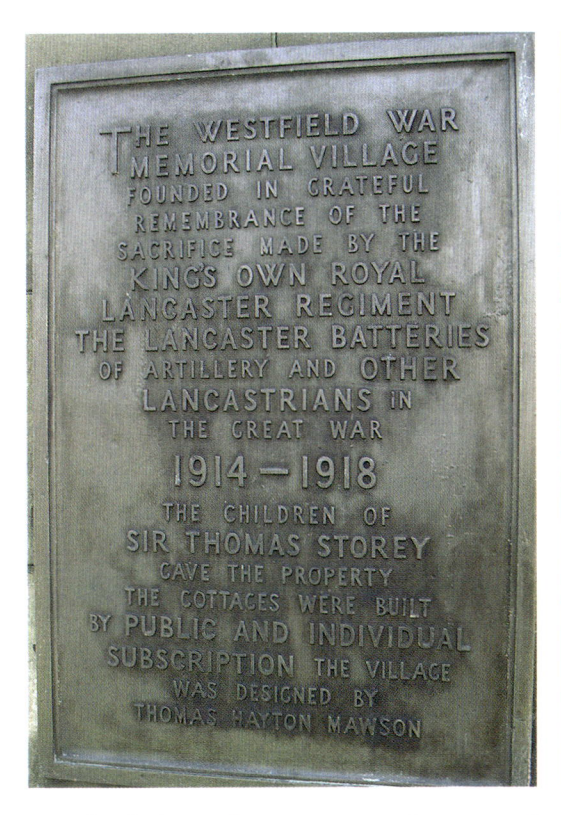

family home for generations, however when Herbert Storey offered the land as a gift and plans were put forward for a village to be built, there was opposition to the scheme. There were those who said that there couldn't be another world war; therefore, the time would come when there wouldn't be any disabled to inhabit the village and the cottages would become derelict. Others even argued on the lines of segregation, adding that men from the battlefields wouldn't want to live with their families in surroundings which would remind them of the horrors of war. The pessimists didn't get very far; their objections were lost in the tide of human determination to do something practical for those who came home scarred by war. So, on a bleak winter's day, Saturday, November 15th, 1919, at 3pm, The Right Honourable Lord Richard Cavendish, CB. CMG., laid the commemorative stone. above the porch of the first cottage, aptly named the Herbert Storey Cottage, of the Westfield Memorial Village, Lancaster.

More cottages, all built from local stone and all paid for by donation, followed; all cottages were named either by, or after, the donor; some were named after battles forever etched in soldiers' hearts. Roads were made; imposing gates were placed at the entrance to this village of memory and a bowling green was added for Mawson was a great believer in fresh air and exercise. To complete the intimacy of this quiet corner of England, which served as a tribute to so much in human sacrifice, they erected a memorial as a centre-piece, a simple statue of a scene from the battlefields; a soldier giving

Cottage in Storey Avenue.

Below Left: Albert Halton VC

Below Right: The Albert Halton Plaque on the house where he lived in Westfield village, Lancaster.

his wounded comrade a drink from his canteen. It had been executed by local artist and sculptor Jenni de la Hunt and unveiled in 1925 by General Sir Archibald Hunter, GCB. On the plinth is a plaque telling anyone who cares to read it, that the village was designed by Thomas Hayton Mawson. There are two other cottages which were more personal still. They were paid for by the family of Lieut. Elsworthy, who was killed in 1917 while serving with the

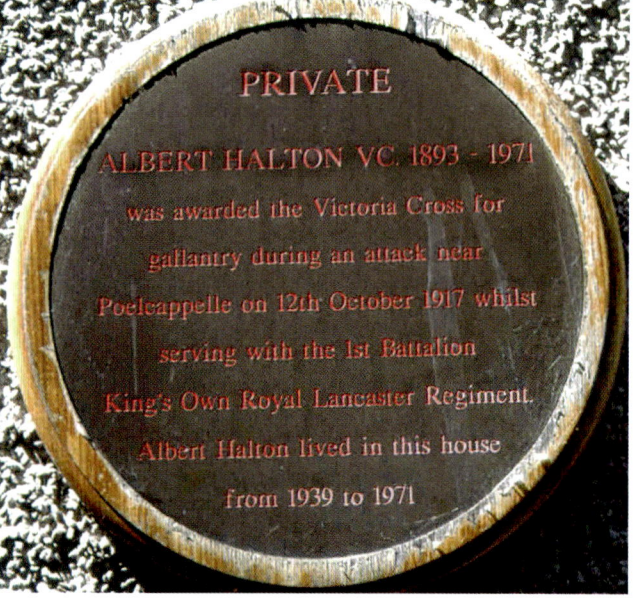

The Storey of the 'Westfield Military Village', Lancaster

The Official Opening on the Bowling Green of Westfield Memorial Village was performed by Field Marshal The Earl Haig

1st. Battalion, the Kings Own Royal Regiment, (Elsworthy Nos. 1 & 2). In one of them lived Albert Halton, VC, Private 1st Battalion The Kings Own (Royal Lancaster) Regiment. As cited in "The Register of the Victoria Cross", "On 12th October 1917 near Poelcapelle, Belgium, after the objective had been reached, Private Halton rushed forward about 300 yards under very heavy fire and captured a machine-gun and its crew which was causing heavy losses to our men. He then went out again and brought in 12 prisoners, showing the greatest disregard for his own safety and setting a fine example to those around him." Born Warton, Carnforth, Lancashire. 1-5-1893. Died Westfield Military Village, Lancaster, 24-7-1971. A small Museum dedicated to Albert Halton now exists on Carnforth railway station. But the kind of men who live in these cottages don't talk easily of things like that, they're just too happy to have enjoyed the life left to them, in peaceful surroundings. They have their own club too, at Westfield,- the gracious large stone house which was the Storey family home for generations and became an addition to the original gift of the land when H. L. Storey's father, Sir Thomas, died. The social life of the community revolves around Westfield and is as strong as the tie which bound the men together on the battlefields, which is just as Thomas Mawson wished it to be.

Westfield, former home of Sir Thomas Storey. Now the Social Club of Westfield village.

The Official Opening of the Village was performed by Field Marshal The Earl Haig, KT, GCB, OM, GCVO, KCIE. on Wednesday, 29th October 1924, at 2-20pm. The Ceremony was held on the Bowling Green in the heart of the village.

After the 2nd World War, the one people said would never happen, the village was expanded and homes with names belonging to that period are seen; Tobruk, Alamein and Arnhem are just a few. So, the disabled of two world wars live together in peace and in surroundings which they themselves say could not be more pleasant. The family name of Storey, as well as that of T. H. Mawson, will have a special place of pride and gratitude in many a soldier's heart.

Cottage named Mons in Westfield.

Chapter 20

MAWSON IN GREECE

Before that however, late in 1917, Mawson learned by 'ticker-tape' that the Greek Parliament had requested him to undertake the re-planning of Salonika, after the Great Fire. This presented rather a predicament for Thomas in regard to the obligations he had undertaken in connection with the industrial villages.

He sought the advice of the Rt. Honourable John Burns, a political leader who, in mid 1914, was one of the very few politicians to foresee the terrible years ahead of the country and, as time unfolded, proving his foresight to be correct, gained the respect of Thomas Mawson. Thomas was urged by John Burns to undertake this work in Salonika, which conferred a great compliment to the profession of town planning as practised in Great Britain and a great honour on Mawson, himself.

It took twelve weeks of communication with the Foreign Office and the War Office to obtain the release of his eldest son (who was engaged upon munitions) and members of his staff whose assistance was essential. The work of securing visas for their passports was also very tedious.

The good result of all this delay was that Thomas had the time, during this period, to complete the propaganda work for the industrial villages, consisting of the study of six proposals as laid down in "An Imperial Obligation". He was then able to leave this work to the Secretary and the Committee, with a clear conscience, and was granted their approval for three months leave.

Thomas was informed that they should travel via Gallipoli on the Italian Peninsula, where they would meet the British Naval Commission and sail by the Greek torpedo destroyer "Panther" which would take them to Piraeus.

After waiting there for two days, the destroyer arrived. There followed a very uncomfortable sea voyage and being aboard "Panther" was both a nauseating and terrifying experience. The very rough sea and the fear of mines and submarines were nothing compared to the corkscrew movements of the boat and its stuffy cabin, but once they arrived at the Corinthian Canal the dangers and discomforts were over.

The first few days of warm welcomings soon passed and, as soon as possible, Thomas and his son, Edward Prentice, called upon Sir George Milne, the British Commander-in-Chief in Salonika. Sir George stated that he was delighted his own countrymen had been engaged to re-plan the town which, even before the fire, had been badly in need of improvement. Sir George found he could assign four young architects to help and, if needed, a good photographer. "Furthermore", he said, "we can do all your blue-prints and reproduce in black line your plans of the town, as you proceed. Finally,

I can place at your disposal a car and a chauffeur!" Thomas had learnt, by letter, that one of his old pupils was in Salonika serving with the military, none other than Harry Pierce, from Windermere! He begged for his release to replace one of the architects.

Harry Pierce had been an eyewitness of the Great Fire of Salonika on August 18th, 1917, and wrote a full account of it, which he had sent to Thomas Mawson.

Viewing the scene, Mawson could see the terrible extent of the havoc the fire had caused and the heart-aching experiences of the poor people. Later in the day Mawson remarked to the Mayor that he had noticed how well the British soldiers seemed to stand with the native population. The Mayor replied, "I am pleased you notice this, for it is a fact, and for very good reason: they are the salt of the earth. I assure you, Mr. Mawson, that on the night of the fire the prestige of the British was raised higher than ever before. Indeed, they did more to strengthen the ties between England and ourselves than your Governments have done in twenty years!"

He went on to tell Thomas of the splendid work that continued throughout the night to save the population. Women and children followed the British soldiers as if they were the natural protectors of these homeless sufferers and these poor people were so grateful to the soldiers that they offered gifts and money. But this gratitude only made the British Tommy sad. He wasn't working for pay... he was simply doing "his bit" and enjoyed doing it. Nothing that Thomas heard in Macedonia pleased him so much as that report from the Mayor.

The first meeting of the commission was held that afternoon, to lay down the rules for the smooth and effective working of several experts. The French members of the commission objected to Mawson being invested with the chairmanship, but all the Greek members, who were in the majority, and not very pleased with the attitude of the French, supported Mawson, and his appointment was duly approved. They decided to discard in large measure that which had already been put forward and study the whole again from start to finish.

Mawson stayed in Salonika for about three months, and during this time was visited by the young King Alexander who took a keen interest in the progress. The Greek Ministers also paid a visit and were so pleased with progress that they invited all the experts and their principal assistants to a very grand lunch at the White Tower Restaurant. The Premier made a most complimentary speech when proposing the health of his guests. As senior member of the commission, it was Mawson's duty to reply. He struck an interesting note by giving a free rendering of a passage from Ruskin: "The greatness of a country does not depend upon the extent of its territory, but upon the number of good men and women within its borders", from which it was meant to infer that the work of the town planners was to provide such conditions as would assure the upbringing and maintenance of good men and women. Thomas was given a hearty handshake by M. Venizelos, the Premier, when he sat down, and asked from where he had got his quotation. Some time later, standing with another Greek minister, the latter pointed to the other side of the road. "See", he said, "there goes M. Venizelos with a volume of Ruskin under his arm". During his stay Mawson was invited to give a number of his lectures on "Industrial Villages for Disabled Service Men", at the depots and halls provided for the men.

At the end of three months, Mawson, his son and staff, in full agreement with their colleagues, had completed a set of thirteen drawings, where every aspect was covered including traffic and fire control. The civic centre, manufacturing and residential areas, parks and boulevards, were all shown. Thomas had also written a very full report, extending to eighty typewritten pages of foolscap.

Although this report was entirely written by Mawson, it was read over in French to the members of the commission and signed by several of them, so that it might go forward as their joint recommendations. A further elaboration for parliamentary approval was completed and the whole went through in three months, a record which was never able to be repeated.

Leaving his eldest son Edward Prentice in control, Thomas started to make his way towards home, calling in Athens on the way. On arrival in Athens, Thomas obtained permission to hold an exhibition of their plans for the capital and Salonika. The plans for Athens occupied two walls of a large room, and the Salonika drawings a third. All were highly praised. At this time, Thomas was joined by his second son, John William, who had been in charge of the Mawson Firm's office in Canada, before the war had started. Joining the military he became an officer in a Canadian regiment. Having been invalided home, he had been granted permission to join his father. Arriving in Athens, he proceeded at once with involvement in the firm's work, assisting the minister in the formulating of building laws and regulations for the rebuilding of Salonika. On completion of the work, he was appointed Director of Reconstruction of the sixty Macedonian villages, which involved the organisation of a very large staff.

On Thomas's arrival in England, he was requested by the Board of Trade Department to the Foreign Office to write a report on the openings for British trade in Macedonia. He had the satisfaction of seeing his report published and circulated by the British Industries Association. The keynote of the report was that "trade followed the town planner". This led to much interviewing and consultation and the forming of powerful groups of British financiers and contractors. Thomas introduced one of these groups to M. Venizelos, who, as a start, gave important contracts for railway and road construction to British firms.

Chapter 21

WITH LORD LEVERHULME IN THE HEBRIDES

In the summer of 1918, there was increasing evidence that this ghastly war was nearly over and many of Mawson's old clients who had put work 'on hold' for the duration began to write about suspended works. His faithful client, Lord Leverhulme, had been High Sheriff of Lancashire from 1917 to 1918, and now had become Mayor of Bolton

Leverhulme, after exploring the Isles of Lewis and Harris in October 1917, when they first came up for sale, formally took possession of Lewis in June 1918 when he returned as Proprietor, having purchased the isle from its owner, Duncan Matheson. Great crowds had turned out to see him and the quay was decorated with a banner which read 'Welcome to Your Island Home'

Early in September of this year, Thomas and his wife Anna were invited to Lews Castle, Stornoway, on the Isle of Lewis, Outer Hebrides, as the guests of Lord and Lady Leverhulme. This was the year when Lever had been created a Baron and chose for his title, Baron Leverhulme (by adding his wife's maiden name to his own) of Bolton-le-Moors.

Lews Castle Stornaway, Outer Hebrides.

Home of Lord and Lady Leverhulme from 1918 until 1923, when Leverhulme gave the castle back to the people of Stornoway.

With Lord Leverhulme in the Hebrides

Stornoway Harbour.

The purchase of the island which was completed on 15th May 1918, was later augmented by the acquisition of neighbouring Isle of Harris in 1919, and various other islands including St. Kilda. Leverhulme and his wife had first visited Stornoway, the chief town of the Isle of Lewis, whilst calling there on a cruise, in August 1884.

Of his invitation Mawson wrote, "I had not been on the island twenty-four hours before I saw I was booked for a very busy fortnight."

Lord Leverhume had already set his fertile brain to work and, organising genius that he was, he looked not only towards the improvement of his own private domain, but also towards the industrial conditions on the island as a whole. The result was that Thomas left Lewis with the data on which to base a report of the natural resources of the island, along with instructions to prepare designs for the castle grounds, and also his lordship's tentative suggestions for the re-planning of the town of Stornoway. These commissions involved an amount of work which kept him busy for the next three months.

Mawson's report, prepared and presented later in the year, planned Lewis as a tourist resort with sporting facilities, especially of loch and river fishing. He suggested the use of peat for fuel, for peat litter and for horticultural purposes; converting peat land into farm and forest lands; creating nursery business for raising and growing young forest trees; osier beds for the development of the basket-making industry; development of small holdings for crofters; soft fruit growing on a large scale; herb growing for drying and distilling; bee-keeping, and experimental research for growth of New Zealand flax.

Mawson wrote of his report presentation: *"After reading it, Lord Leverhulme jocularly described me as the most imaginative man he had ever met."*

Some work at Lews Castle was carried out on the grounds. The Matheson's walled kitchen garden was transformed into eight terraces, and a tennis court was laid out between this and the castle, the work probably being planned by Edward Prentice Mawson who was also invited to stay there with his wife.

Unfortunately, trouble among the locals, like a series of farm raids, reared up and as a result Leverhulme moved his centre of attention from Stornoway to Obbe, renamed Leverbourgh in his honour, apparently at the wish of its inhabitants. On Harris, he made a final desperate bid to make his schemes work. Leverhume's residence on this island was called "Borve Lodge", on the west coast. A circular, walled kitchen garden, similar in conception to his early design at Thornton Manor, was formed, adorned with statues and a sundial, identical to one which stood in front of Lews Castle, and may be the same one, having been brought to "Borve Lodge" when Leverhume left Stornoway.

Following this failure with Lewis, some years later Lord Leverhume offered the Island, upon which he had from the first to last spent over a million pounds stirling, as a gift to the Islanders, but this offer was refused; and yet the refusal is not difficult to understand. The tenant of a croft paid ten shillings a year rent, and his landlord paid the rates. This amounted to sixpence more than the rent, so why should the tenant (and a Scotsman at that) turn landlord and lose his sixpence a year?

Chapter 22

THE ARMISTICE

The Armistice, which officially ended the First World War, was signed on the eleventh hour of the eleventh day of the eleventh month of 1918.

It brought into practical operation much work for private individuals. Very soon, the housing of the working classes became the slogan of every political party. The cries were for "Houses fit for heroes to live in." Every authority, be it council, borough, or urban district was invited to estimate its needs and to present schemes for the approval of the Ministry which would grant a liberal subsidy. So urgent was the supply of additional houses regarded, that their Majesties the King George V and Queen Mary, accompanied by the Prince of Wales and Princess Mary, supplemented the efforts of their Ministers by giving a reception at Buckingham Palace, on April 11th, 1919.

All public bodies and the National Housing and Town Planning Council were invited to send representatives. Thomas H. Mawson was one of the chosen delegates.

In all there were about five hundred people present. The group which included Thomas Mawson was introduced to the Royalty by Mr. Henry Aldridge. The atmosphere was electric,…watching these masters of royal courtesy making their guests at ease, saying a word here and a word there. When the time came for Thomas to be introduced to the King, Mr. Aldridge presented him as the re-planner of Athens. The King cordially shook his hand and Thomas then passed on, as did the others, to shake hands with the Queen. He was delighted when, as she shook his hand, she told him, quite simply, *'she had been following his work with interest,'* and with apparent appreciation.

Later, in His Majesty's Address, one paragraph which Thomas remembered in particular was; *"It is not merely 'houses' that are needed. The new houses must also be 'homes'. Can we not aim at securing to the working classes in their homes the comfort, leisure, brightness and peace which we usually associate with the word 'home'?"* Great applause.

The housing boom was now in full swing and Mawson was commissioned by the Wood Green Council, who had acquired the Cline Estate (fifty acres) and the White Hart estate of forty acres, both excellent sites for their purpose, to prepare lay-out plans. Site plans were made showing 450 houses for the first, and 432 houses for the other, after approval by the Ministry of Health.

Only fifty houses were built before Dr. Addison was replaced as Minister of Health by Sir Alfred Mond, who reversed his predecessor's policy and practically brought housing to a standstill. The results attained fell short by at least eighty per cent of what politicians had advocated as a minimum necessity. One of the reasons given was the greed amongst builders, merchants and manufacturers to force up the prices. In the early stages, this was unfortunately true.

Problems were also arising in Greece, which necessitated a return visit by Thomas, accompanied by his wife and daughter-in-law, the wife of Edward Prentice, who had already been in Greece for several months in charge of the work out there, along with his brother, John, who had been compiling the conditions of sale and building ordnances for Salonika, for several months.

The Greek situation seemed to go on and on. Mawson began to learn that what a Greek said and what a Greek did were two different things. He was constantly aware that the time spent in Greece was keeping him more and more away from work in England. Already, this Greek work was monopolising the entire energies of his two sons and nearly half of his own time too. He knew that, eventually, he would have to choose between England or Greece.

English work was coming in fast, too, and Mawson was invited to prepare a comprehensive town-planning scheme for Northhampton.

Soon after receiving the Northampton work, Thomas was called to be a consultant to advise the Windermere Urban District Council to work in collaboration with its very able surveyor, Mr. Charles Hines, to solve certain increasingly difficult traffic conditions on approaching Windermere from the south.

It will interest motorists to know that in the report they recommended a road which would avoid the two steep hills encountered upon entering Windermere from the south by branching off left in the direction of the lake after leaving the hamlet of Ings.

Passing along in front of Black Moss Farm, it would join the high road to the lake at Queen's Drive, halfway between Windermere and Bowness. Another bypass road to avoid congestion in the lower part of Bowness could branch off at the top of Crag Brow, passing behind the Crown Hotel and joining up with the Kendal and Newby Bridge route at a convenient point clear of the village. All this planning would be done around the year 1919 but no action was taken, either then or since and, all these years later, traffic into Windermere from the south still comes to a standstill on those very same two hills!

Late 1919 saw further progress in the post-war reorganisation of the Mawson Practice. Old members of the staff resumed their accustomed work and pupils, whose studies had been interrupted by war, returned to complete their tuition. Old and new clients for both public and private projects were filling the office with interesting work.

The Armistice

Dunira near Comrie Perthshire, Scotland.

Home of William Gilchrist Macbeth c. 1920.

The two most attractive schemes were Boveridge Park in Cranbourne, Dorset, and Dunira near Comrie in Perthshire.

Dunira had recently been purchased by well-known shipowner, Mr. William Gilchrist Macbeth. At this time, considerable work in alterations and

Formal Gardens at Dunira.

93

additions to the house were being carried out. Thomas wrote, *"Dunira is one of the most beautiful estates it has ever been my pleasure to study. The Park, which extends to many hundreds of acres, is perfectly level, and the soil a rich alluvial deposit. Out of this plain arises somewhat precipitously a number of high mounds which suggest that these were at one time islands and promontories rising out of a lake, much in the same way as Windermere and its islands; in fact, when mist lies out over the park it is very easy to imagine a large lake studded with wooded islands. Beyond these islands are forest-clad mountains which completely encircle the estate, but at such a distance as to create an aspect of spaciousness. The encircling range of mountains reminded me of Grasmere as seen from Dunmail Raise, only they were even more picturesque in their rugged outlines and towering peaks, whilst everywhere the slopes and foothills were clothed with timber wherein groupings of Scotch firs gave a massive effect to the whole".*

It was to this lovely estate, which so much reminded Mawson of his beloved Lake District, that he sent one of his promising young workers from Windermere, William Reed, a local Windermere man, born and bred, and made him foreman in charge of laying out the gardens of Dunira in accordance with the plans drawn by Thomas Mawson. Bill Reed, as he was known, lived and worked at Dunira for two years, c1920-22, and loved it every bit as much as Mawson did, so much so, that when he returned to Windermere and married, he called his own house 'Dunira'.

Dunira at Windermere former home of Bill Reed, who was Mawson foreman gardener at Dunira, Perthshire.

Thomas Mawson, meanwhile, was called to return to Athens once more, leaving Dunira under the direction of his skilled landscape foremen and son, Edward Prentice, latterly returned from Athens for a rest.

The Armistice

A telegram from Mawson's second son, John, who was in charge of the Macedonian Reconstruction, warning his father of a threatened possible strike by the forty English engineers of the work force had been received.

A strike had taken place because of appalling delays to the work, for which the men were holding John responsible. His father called a conference and John spoke to the men for over an hour, telling them of the frustrations and disappointments he himself had had to bear. He told them of the entire lack of support which he had received from the Greek Government and had, in fact, put in his own resignation.

What interest could there be in planning a noble park system so long as the Government could ill afford to even pay for the plans, much less spend money in constructing and planting the parks.

These types of problems, coupled with the swift depreciation of the drachma, caused Thomas to start packing, ready to return home. Before he could leave, however, he received a request to attend the Ministry the next morning. Mildly surprised, he did so and was greeted by a number of friendly officials. Thomas was then quaintly informed that he was to receive a mark of the King's favour.

The prime Minister made a warm congratulatory address, thanking Thomas for his work in Salonika and his preliminary scheme for the replanning and extension of Athens. He then presented Thomas with the Order of the Saviour, (a gold clasp), and onlookers applauded loudly. M. Papanastassiou then added that he would like also to present the Order of King George to Mawson's eldest son, Edward Prentice Mawson, for the help he had given to his father and to the people of Greece.

With a promise to return to Athens as soon as there was sufficient progress to justify it, Thomas said goodbye to the young King, whom he was never to see again, and to the Ministers and the many friends he had made. Unfortunately, the drachma depreciated to such an extent that practically all public works were stopped.

Another consequence of this was that now Mawson's second son, John William, was also free for new projects and, at this point, he emigrated to New Zealand and became Town Planning Consultant to the New Zealand Government.

Chapter 23

CHANGES IN 1920

Caton, Lancashire.

'The Fish Steps', belonging to Caton Hall, where the Evangelist John Wesley, once preached to village people from miles around on his itinerant Tour, c. 1770.

Eagerly looking forward to coming home for a quiet rest at the shore-line bungalow at Hest Bank, described by Thomas as *"On the shore, with two acres of lawn running down to the bay, and miles of yellow and light brown sand alternating with tidal waters, stretching away into blue and green distances, backed by the Lakeland Mountains"*, he was shattered to find that his wife had sold the beloved bungalow, which really belonged to her, and bought Caton Hall, as a surprise for him.

Situated in the village of Caton, near Lancaster, in the valley of the River Lune, Caton Hall stood in eleven acres of finely timbered grounds, three of which were an old-world garden and eight a small park. Its situation gave fine views to the north, west and south and was screened by a fine high wall to the east, on which lay the village.

The thing about Caton Hall, of which Thomas was most proud, was its connection with John Wesley, the Evangelist, of which he says, *"Close by the entrance is an oak tree with fish steps bordering a stream at its base, and from these steps, John Wesley preached on one of his itinerant tours. It is not difficult to portray the slight reverent figure of this evangelist, in his customary black gown and white Geneva bib, surrounded by an awed crowd of villagers at this picturesque corner. The tree and the steps are part of the property"*.

The sandstone steps were used by the monks from Cockeram Abbey to display and sell fish caught in the River Lune, and the oak tree was planted to give shade. Both still remain near the entrance to Caton Hall, although the oak tree, now a tremendous age, is held erect by a tall iron stake.

Post-war work on previous designs at Rivington for Lord Leverhulme re-

Changes in 1920

The Dell Rivington.

Above Left: The construction of the waterfall.

Above Right: The finished waterfall.

Left: The straight bridge in The Dell.

commenced. It consisted of building two stone bridges across a chasm, one arched, one straight, and making a series of cascades with a total fall of over two hundred feet. This area was known as the Dell. They were able to divert several smaller streams to argument the construction of a pond as a compensation reservoir capable of supplying an additional half million gallons against dry weather to the reservoirs.

About this time, Mawson suffered what the doctor described as a slight seizure, and he was advised to take a complete rest for six months. This was absolutely foreign to his nature and he was in daily communication with his office, gradually resuming his unstoppable interest in the firm's work.

He had noticed at this time, an article by Mr. Ernest Lawson on "Town Planning for Blackpool" which appeared in the "Blackpool Herald" in which the writer advised that the firm of 'Mawson' should be consulted. This came as a surprise to Thomas, who had never communicated with Blackpool in any way. He awaited further developments and finally, in July 1922, received a letter from the Town Clerk of Blackpool informing Thomas that his Council had purchased two hundred and eighty acres of land for a park and recreation ground and wished to consult the Mawson Firm upon its development.

Thomas realised that his thoughts on the re-planning of Blackpool was now a distinct possibility and would call for the application of town-planning principles of which he was a past master.

The commission led to being asked to plan the new South Shore extension which included a new promenade about a mile in length. This was to be reclaimed from the sea and protected by a stout sea wall, which would form the boundary along the promenade. The distance would extend from the open-air swimming baths southwards towards the junction with the borough of St. Anne's, including the sandhills on the shoreline.

The spacious promenade extended along in a gentle curve with all the gardens being protected from the sea breezes by being sunk two feet below the surface and causing a pleasing effect from the main thoughfare which is crowded by day and night by pedestrians. The brilliant lighting of the promenade by night is a special feature of the scheme. (The beginning of the famous 'Illuminations', perhaps?)

The planning of Stanley Park, in Blackpool, was also included.

More localised planning was still going ahead too, and the name of Thomas H. Mawson and son, High Street House, Lancaster, was stamped upon the plans of the lovely house known as "Broomhill", in Birthwaite Road, Windermere, on July 27th, 1922, for Dr. A. E. Barclay.

Broomhill, designed by T.H. Mawson and son. Note the slated gable.

Also in 1922, Baron Leverhulme became a Viscount and chose as his title, Viscount Leverhulme of the Western Isles.

Chapter 24

THE FINAL YEARS

Thomas and Anna stayed at Caton Hall only a few years before Thomas designed what was to be his final home, "Applegarth", back at Hest Bank again. Strangely, "Applegarth did not follow the well known characteristics of most of his previous house designs. There was not a slated apex in sight, as in the house neighbouring to "Applegarth", known as "Brackondale", designed and built for Edward Prentice Mawson, many years earlier. It was more rectangular and plain, with the only familiar Mawson feature being the large flat lawn at the rear reached by descending, wide spreading steps.

Front of Applegarth, Hest Bank.

Rear of Applegarth, Hest Bank showing lawn and spreading steps.

As his energies decreased, his sons accepted heavier duties with courage and ability, and a freshness of outlook which made their father happy in the thought of future prospects. Thomas had maintained for some years that if the training of the garden designer has included the study of domestic architecture, and if in consequence he is entrusted with the design of both house and garden, he may accomplish greater artistic results than he has ever dreamed of.

Of his three daughters, Thomas very much regretted denying them the same opportunities which the boys were given. Never the less, at Thornton Hall in Lincolnshire, home of Colonel Smethhurst and husband of Helen, elder daughter of Thomas and Anna, the sisters established Thornton Art Industries. Here, surrounded by a band of lady workers they turned out a considerable quantity of useful and ornamental articles. From the start their business met with encouragement and became well established.

With the death of his great friend and best client, Lord Leverhulme, on 7th May 1925, Thomas felt a great loss. The old days,...the good days were gone, only to be relived in precious memories.

The last great effort Thomas Mawson had made, to keep the records straight, was to write his autobiography, which was published in 1926, and towards its close he wrote;-

> *"Experience has taught me that the world is much more kindly than some affirm, and that it admires above all things courage and tenacity. Men and women who love trees and flowers are ever pleasant and understanding company, and my deepest regret is that I no longer possess the energy to tramp the road with them. Yet in imagination I am still walking with my clients through the gardens I have helped to create, picturing the development of succeeding years, but regretful that I cannot curb wayward growths or re-organise and amend those portions which have fallen short of expectation...for a garden, like a family, has to be' brought up' and needs constant care if its character is to be developed. To me the garden and its design are still my highest pleasure. The green shades are my keenest delight and my estimate of the ethical value of a garden is well expressed by Wordsworth in the following lines;-*
> *'A garden.........the place*
> *Where good men disappointed in the quest*
> *Of wealth and power and honours, long for rest;*
> *Or having known the splendours of success,*
> *Sigh for the obscurities of happiness.'*
> *Like my friend Daniel Burnam, 'I feel I have done a day's work'*
> *.........and there is great satisfaction in the thought!"*

It was here, at Applegarth, that Thomas died on 14th November 1933, aged 72 years.

The Final Years

Prior to his internment in Bowness-on-Windermere Cemetery, within a few miles of some of his best gardens, a Service was held in Hest Bank Congregational Church.

This was an appropriate place because it had been designed by Mawson's former colleague and friend, Dan Gibson, and Thomas had, himself, been involved in the interior work. His wife, daughters and ladies of the parish had proudly kept the inside immaculate, always.

The pretty little church so beloved by Mawson, with its air of peace and tranquillity and the commanding view across Morcambe Bay stretching to the Lakeland mountains beyond, was crowded to capacity.

The congregation was, for the most part, composed of local residents. They had gathered together to pay their last tribute of respect to the memory of one who had endeared himself to all with whom he came into contact. His former devoted employee and faithful friend, Mr. James Crossland, attended.

The profusion of floral tributes, however, included wreaths from various organisations with which Thomas Mawson was identified, and there were many from foreign countries around the world.

The view from Hest Bank across Morecambe Bay to the Lakeland hills which Thomas Mawson loved so much.

HONOURS BESTOWED ON THOMAS HAYTON MAWSON

Liveryman of the Worshipful Company of Gardeners.

Lecturer on Civic Design to the University of Liverpool.

Doyen of the International Commission for the Re-Building of Salonika.

Order of the Redeemer. (Greece, first class)

Fellow of the Linnaean Society.

Member and President of the Town Planning Institute 1923-24.

First President of the newly formed Institute of Landscape Architects, 1929.

Member of the National Housing and Town Planning Council.

Honorary Corresponding Member of the American Society of Landscape Architects.

Member of the Royal Arboricultural Society of Scotland.

A Founder Member of the Royal Fine Arts Commission.

After Thomas Hayton Mawson's retirement, his son, Edward Prentice Mawson carried on the firm and became a President of the Institute of Landscape Architects, of which his father was the First President.

LIST OF PUBLICATIONS BY T. H. MAWSON

Hanley Park, Hanley. 1894

The Art and Craft of Garden Making. 5 Editions.
1900, 1901, 1907, 1912 and 1926.

Civic Art; Studies in Town Planning, Parks, Boulevards and Open Spaces.

The City of Calgary, Past, Present and Future. 1914.

Exeter of the Future.
A policy of improvement within a period of one hundred years.

Borden Park, Ottawa.
A report on the development of the new suburb.

Bolton as it is and as it might be.
Six lectures on Town Planning.

Bolton.
A study in Town Planning and Civic Art

Dunfermline.
An illustrated report prepared for the Carnegie Dunfermline Trust.

Athens of the Future.

Blackpool Park and Recreational Centre.

Northampton.
A scheme of Civic Development and Expansion.

An Imperial Obligation.
Industrial Villages for Disabled Service Men.

The Life and Work of an English Landscape Architect.
(Dedicated to his Wife.)

ACKNOWLEDGEMENTS

My grateful thanks go to:
Margaret Thomas, Vice Chairman, Lakeland Horticultural Society.
Thomas Prentice Mawson, Grandson.
Andrea Rollins, Great Gandaughter.
United Utilities, Great House Information Centre, Rivington. Special thanks to Sue Harper.
M. D. Smith, Rivington research.
Ken Hughes. Lakeland Horticultural Society colleague.
'Brockhole', Lake District National Park. Special thanks to Susan Fryer, Head Gardener.
Anthony H. Gaddum, descendant of the Gaddums of 'Brockhole'.
Marjorie & John Harrison, Mawson Garden and rare photograph.
Beth & Rod Davies, Mawson Garden.
Dorothy & Jack Jackson, Mawson Garden.
Mr. & Mrs. Roberts, Mawson Garden.
Heather & Alan Rhodes, Mawson Garden.
Thelma & Uter Potter, Mawson House.
Vivienne Ford, Mawson Garden & old photographs.
Patricia Murphy, Dan Gibson House.
Steve Warbrick, Director of Regeneration, Barrow-in-Furness.
Derek Lyon, Town Clerk, Rtd. Barrow-in-Furness.
Bill Brown, Parks Manager, Barrow-in-Furness.
John Winder, Chartered Accountant, Barrow-in-Furness.
Chris Jones, Eskdale. Leader of 'lost Japanese garden' restoration.
John Reed, descendant Mawson Staff, and Colin Tyson, Bowness historian.
John O'Hara, 'Armitt Library' colleague.
Mr. & Mrs. S. Crabtree, rare photograph.
Mr. Peter Naylor, Mawson Walled Garden.
Henry Noblett, Founder member and past President of Lakeland Horticultural Society.
David Mawson, OBE DL Grandson.
Nigel Crook. I T.

And last, but not least, my husband Harry, who has had to live with Thomas Mawson for the past five years, as well as me!

Photographing all the lovely gardens I have mentioned, and meeting the kind and helpful owners, (who have now become my friends) including the persons who so willingly helped me with the loan of books and old photographs, has, for me, been a privilege and a pleasure for which they have my deepest gratitude. Thank you all!   Bette Kissack.